Racism Explained to My Daughter

Racism Explained to My Daughter

TAHAR BEN JELLOUN

With responses from

WILLIAM AYERS, LISA D. DELPIT,

DAVID MURA,

and **PATRICIA WILLIAMS**

Introduction by **BILL COSBY**

THE NEW PRESS

LIBRARY OF CONGRESS CATALOGING-IN-PUBLICATION DATA

Ben Jelloun, Tahar, 1944–
    [Racism expliqué à ma fille. English]
    Racism explained to my daughter / Tahar Ben Jelloun ;
translated from the French by Carol Volk ; with responses by
William Ayers ... [et al.] ; introduction by Bill Cosby.
    p. cm.
    Rev. translation of: Racism expliqué à ma fille.
    ISBN 1-56584-534-x (Hardcover)
    1. Racism. 2. Race awareness in children. 3. Prejudices in children.
    1. Title.
HT1521.B39813 1999
305.8 – dc21   98-33183
OCLC #40403581   CIP

A modified version of "Racism Explained to My Daughter"
was published in France by Editions du Seuil
as *Le racisme expliqué à ma fille.*

Published in the United States by The New Press, New York
Distributed by W. W. Norton & Company, Inc., New York

*The New Press was established in 1990 as a not-for-profit alternative
to the large, commercial publishing houses currently dominating
the book publishing industry. The New Press operates in the public interest
rather than for private gain, and is committed to publishing,
in innovative ways, works of educational, cultural, and community value
that are often deemed insufficiently profitable.*

www.thenewpress.com
Book design by BAD
Printed in the United States of America
9 8 7 6 5 4 3 2 1

Contents

Acknowledgments

I would like to thank my friends
who were kind enough to read my words
and share their thoughts with me.

Thanks also to Mérième's friends
who helped shape the questions.

TAHAR BEN JELLOUN

Introduction

BILL COSBY

IN THE EARLY 1900s, the great African American scholar and activist W.E.B. Du Bois predicted that the problem of the color line would turn out to be the twentieth century's critical challenge. By the 1960s, many of us believed that the civil rights movement could eliminate racism in America during our lifetime. But despite significant progress, racism remains. In both its hidden and open forms, it continues to be a serious problem for the United States. It persists as the ugly precursor of genocide in many other countries. As we approach the millennium, *Racism Explained to My Daughter* is, unfortunately, an all-too-timely work.

Tahar Ben Jelloun, a French writer of Moroccan background, began this book in response to his ten-year-old daughter's question, "What is racism?" It is a thoughtful answer to a complicated question; the language is simplified, but the text is comprehensive. The discussion ranges from discrimination to xenophobia (meaning the fear of foreigners) as Ben Jelloun talks about color and cultural differences, genetics, the major religions, colonialism, and stereotypes. Along the way, he reminds readers that racism is a bane of the human species around the world, a bane that has poisoned societies for centuries. It turns individuals against each other, causing physical and psychological harm to millions of people. It leads nations to scapegoat entire populations, resulting in the horrors of genocide. Racism, one of our deepest flaws as humans, is ultimately a threat to our survival.

It is disheartening to see that children are still shaped by racism — racism that these children learn from parents, relatives, and friends in lessons reinforced by the media and society at large. Ben Jelloun lets young readers know that they should not let themselves be bullied by racist children or adults, or be made to feel inferior by narrow-minded people. Instead, they should realize that racists themselves are deeply troubled and in need of healing, for racism is an illness. It is a statement some readers may find extreme. But it needs to be said, because racism cannot be accepted as normal in any society: such a view promotes intolerance in individuals and nations. Without mincing words, he also describes racists as cowards suffering from feelings of inferiority (or exaggerated superiority), feelings that make them afraid of other people who are "different." Racism is an evil, he says flatly, that "comes out of fear, ignorance and stupidity."

As it strips away layer after layer, *Racism Explained to My Daughter* will sharpen our understanding of racism's social, economic, political, and psychological dimensions. Tahar Ben Jelloun earnestly wants young people to appreciate the complexities of racism so they will be prepared to root it out, both in themselves and in others. Passivity will not do. Children and adults, he argues, must have the courage to stand up and struggle against racism—every day, if necessary.

I like his approach. We need to raise a new generation to be free of prejudice. We owe it to them, and to humanity. Children who read this book will be rewarded with insight and hope. Adults will, too.

Tahar Ben Jelloun with his daughter

Racism Explained to My Daughter

TAHAR BEN JELLOUN

The idea for this book came to me on February 22, 1997, the day my daughter and I went to protest the Debré law, a law dealing with foreigners' rights in France.* My ten-year-old daughter asked question after question. She wanted to know why we were demonstrating, what certain slogans meant, if protesting would do any good.

That's how we began to talk about racism. I wrote this book as I thought about her questions. When I was done, we read it together. Then I rewrote it almost entirely, changing difficult words and explaining hard concepts. Next we read it again with two of her friends. Their reactions were also valuable, so I added them to subsequent revisions.

This text was rewritten at least fifteen times. It had to be clear, simple, and objective. I wanted it to be accessible to everyone, even though I wrote it mainly for children ages eight to fourteen.

* See page 78.

The basic idea is that the fight against racism begins with education. Children can be educated more easily than adults. That's why I wrote this book.

Daddy, what is racism?

Racism is a common phenomenon that occurs in every society. Unfortunately, it has become quite common in certain countries, where it exists without anyone even thinking about it. It consists of being mistrustful of people, even looking down on those who have physical and cultural characteristics different from your own.

When you say it's "common," do you mean it's normal?

No, just because it's common doesn't mean it's normal. In general, people are wary of those who are different from themselves—foreigners, for example. This kind of attitude is as old as mankind. It's universal.

If it's universal, could I be racist?

Well, children aren't usually racist by nature. No one is born racist. If your parents or the people around you don't put racist ideas in your head, there's no reason you should become so. But if you're led to believe that people with white skin are superior to people with dark skin, and if you take this idea seriously, you might have a racist attitude toward blacks.

What does "superiority" mean?

It means, for example, that because you have white skin, you think you're more intelligent than someone whose skin is another color—black or yellow. But in fact our body's physical traits, which distinguish us from each other, do not imply any inequality.

Do you think I could become a racist?

It's possible. It all depends on what you've been taught. It's better to be aware and stop yourself from being one, to accept the idea that any child or any adult is capable— in thought or deed—of rejecting someone who hasn't done anything wrong but who is simply different. This happens a lot. Anyone can behave cruelly or have nasty thoughts. Someone we don't know might annoy us.

We decide either that we're better than that person or that that person is better than we are, and we reject the person — we don't want him for a neighbor, much less a friend, simply because he's different.

Different?

When you say someone is different, you mean they don't resemble you.

We say people are "different" because their skin is a different color, because they speak another language, eat different food, have different customs, a different religion, different ways of living, of celebrating, and so on. There are differences in physical appearance (height, skin color, facial features), and then there are differences in behavior, ways of thinking, beliefs and other things.

Does that mean racists don't like languages, food, or skin colors different from their own?

No, not exactly. Racists might like learning other languages because they need them for work or for travel, but they might judge the people who speak these languages in an unfair and negative way. Or, they might not want to rent a room to a foreign student, say, a Vietnamese student, and yet they might love Vietnamese food. A racist is someone who thinks that anything different threatens his peaceful existence.

Racists feel threatened?

Yes, they're afraid of anyone who's not like them. Racists have either inferiority or superiority complexes. It doesn't matter which one; either way, they look down on the other person.

They're afraid?

People need to feel secure. They don't like to have their ideas questioned. People are often afraid of what they don't know. We're afraid of the dark because we don't know what might happen to us when the lights go out. We feel helpless in the face of the unknown. We imagine terrible things for no reason — it's not logical. Sometimes we know our fear is totally unfounded, but we're afraid anyway. No matter how hard we try to be reasonable, we act as if the threat were real. Racism is not something real or reasonable.

Daddy, if racists are afraid, that politician* who doesn't like foreigners must be afraid all the time. But every time he's on television, I'm the one who's afraid. He yells and threatens the interviewer and bangs on the table.

Yes, but the party leader you're talking about is a politician who's known for being extremely aggressive. His racism is expressed as violence. He lies to people who don't know any better so they'll be afraid. He exploits the real fear people sometimes feel. For example, he tells them that immigrants come to France to take French people's jobs, collect welfare, and get free health care. It's not true. Immigrants often do the jobs French people don't want to do. They pay taxes and social security; they have a right to medical care when they get sick. If, God forbid, they expelled all the immigrants from France tomorrow, the economy would crumble.

* Jean-Marie Le Pen, founder of the National Front Party in France

I see. Racists are afraid for no reason.

They're afraid of foreigners, of people they don't know, especially if the foreigner is poor. They'd be more wary of an African worker than of an American billionaire. When an Arab sheik vacations on the Riviera, he's welcomed with open arms, because he's not considered an "Arab" but a rich man ready to spend his money.

What's a foreigner?

The word "foreigner" comes from the word "foreign," which means "from the outside." It means someone who's not part of the family, who doesn't belong to the clan or the tribe. A foreigner is someone who comes from another country—it can be nearby or far away—or sometimes just from another city or village. This is where we get the word "xenophobia," which means being hostile to foreigners, to anyone who comes from a foreign country. Today the word "foreign" suggests something odd, something different from what we're used to seeing. It's almost a synonym for "strange."

When I go to my friend's house in Normandy, am I a foreigner?

To the locals, probably, yes, because you come from somewhere else, from Paris, and you're Moroccan. Do you remember when we went to Senegal? To the Senegalese, we were "foreigners."

But the Senegalese weren't afraid of us, and I wasn't afraid of them!

That's right, because your mother and I explained to you that you shouldn't be afraid of foreigners, rich or poor, old or young, white or black. Don't forget: You're always a foreigner to someone. That is, someone not from your culture will always think of you as "foreign."

Daddy, I still don't understand why racism exists everywhere.

A long time ago, in primitive societies, people acted more instinctively, like animals. A cat marks its territory. If another cat, or another animal, tries to steal its food or take its young, the cat uses its claws to defend itself and protect its young. People are like that, too. They like to have their own house, their land, their possessions. There's nothing unusual about that. But racists think that foreigners, no matter who they are, are going to take things away from them. As a result, they're mistrustful of them, almost instinctively. Animals don't fight unless they're attacked. But sometimes people attack foreigners, even when the foreigners had no intention of taking anything from them.

And this happens in every society?

It happens, but that doesn't mean it's natural. People have behaved this way for centuries. There's nature and there's culture. There's instinctive behavior, which means acting without thinking or reasoning, and then there's reasoned behavior, which we develop through education, school, and logic. That's what we call "culture," as opposed to "nature." Culture teaches us to live together, teaches us that we're not alone in the world, that other people have different traditions and ways of living that are just as valid as our own.

If culture means education, can racism come from what we learn?

No one is born a racist; you become one. What you learn can be good or bad. It depends on who's doing the teaching, at school or at home.

So animals are better than people, even though they're not educated?

Well, let's just say that animals don't have preconceived notions. But people have what are called prejudices. They judge others without knowing them. They think they know in advance what other people are like and if they're worthwhile or not. Often they're wrong. That's where their fear comes from. People even go to war to fight their fears. When I say people are afraid, it's not that they're paralyzed with fear; just the opposite. Some people attack when they feel threatened. Racists can be aggressive.

So racism causes wars?

Some wars, yes. At the core, there's a desire to take what someone else has. Racism is used to convince people to hate each other even though they don't know each other. People are afraid of foreigners, afraid they'll take their houses, their jobs, their families. Ignorance breeds fear. You don't know the foreigner, and the foreigner doesn't know you. Think about our neighbors. They were stand-offish for a long time, until we invited them over to eat couscous with us. Then they realized we were just like them. Once they knew us, we didn't seem dangerous any-more, even though we're from another country—Moroc-co. By inviting them over, we got rid of their fears. We talked, we got to know each other better. We laughed together. That meant we felt comfortable with each other, whereas before, when we passed each other on the stairs, we barely said hello.

So to fight racism, people should invite each other over!

It's a good idea. Getting to know people, talking, laughing, sharing your joys, but also your sorrows, realizing that people often have the same concerns, the same problems, all that could make racism go away. Traveling is also a good way to get to know people better. As early as the sixteenth century, the French philosopher Michel de Montaigne encouraged his countrymen to travel and experience different cultures. For him, travel was the best way to "rub and sharpen our minds against those of others." The more we know about other people, the more we know about ourselves.

Has racism always existed?

Yes, from the beginning of man's existence racism has appeared in different forms. In prehistoric times, men attacked each other with clubs and weapons over a piece of land, a hut, a woman, and food. To protect themselves against an invasion, they began building barriers and preparing weapons. People are obsessed with security, and this can lead them to be afraid of their neighbors—foreigners.

Is racism war?

Wars have different causes, some of which are economic. But some wars are fought to assert the supposed superiority of one group over another. Education and reason can combat this kind of thinking. But for this to work, people have to decide to stop being afraid of their neighbors, of foreigners.

So what can we do?

We can learn, we can educate ourselves and we can think. We can try to understand things, to be curious about everything that affects people, to control our instincts and impulses.

What's an impulse?

It's acting without thinking. It's related to the word "repulse," which means to push away, as in chasing out an enemy. To be repulsed can also mean to be disgusted. It's very negative.

Racists try to get rid of foreigners because they're disgusted by them?

Yes, sometimes they try to chase them even out if they don't feel threatened, but simply don't like them. To justify their behavior, they'll use any argument. Sometimes they use science, but science has never justified racism. They make science say what they want it to say, because they think science provides inarguable proof. Racism has no basis in science, even though people have tried to use it to justify their ideas of discrimination.

What does discrimination mean?

Singling out one social or ethnic group for harsh treatment. For example, if a school decided to put all the black students in one class because it considered these children less intelligent than the others. Fortunately, this kind of discrimination doesn't exist in French schools. It existed in American schools until the 1960s and in South Africa until recently. When you force a community—whether it's an ethnic community or a religious one—to live apart from the rest of the population, you create what is called a ghetto.

Is that a prison?

"Ghetto" is actually the name of a little island near Venice, in Italy. In 1516, the Jews of Venice were sent to this island, to isolate them from other communities. A ghetto is a type of a prison. In any case, it's discrimination.

What do racists use as their "scientific proof"?

There's no such thing as "scientific proof" for racism. Racists believe—and try to make others believe—that foreigners belong to another race, an inferior race. But they're completely wrong; there's only one race, the human race, unlike the animal kingdom, in which there are great differences from one species to the next. For example, there is the canine species and the bovine species. Within the canine species, the differences are so large (think of a German sheperd compared to a Chihuahua) that it's possible to define "races." For the human race, this is impossible, because all men are equal.

But Daddy, people talk about the white race, the black race, or the yellow race. We hear that at school. The teacher told us the other day that Abdou's race was black. He's from Mali.

If your teacher really said that, she was wrong. I hate to tell you this, because I know you like her, but she's wrong and I think she doesn't even know it. Human races don't exist. There is a human species in which there are men and women, people of color, tall people and short people, with different strengths and weaknesses. And there are several animal races. The word "race" shouldn't be used to distinguish differences among humans. The word "race" has no scientific basis. People use it to exaggerate differences in physical appearance. But we shouldn't use physical differences— skin color, height, facial features—to divide humanity hierarchically, that is, to claim that some people are better than others. In other words, no one has the right to think, or to make others think, that because his skin is white he is "better" than a person of color. I suggest you stop using the word "race." It's been so exploited by bad people that it's better to replace it with the word humanity. The human species is composed of various groups, but all men and women on this planet have the same color blood in their veins, whether their skin is pink, white, black, brown, yellow, or anything else.

Why do Africans have black skin and Europeans white skin?

Skin color is determined by a pigment called melanin. This pigment exists in all human beings, but Africans have more of it than Europeans or Asians.

So my friend Abdou makes more...

Melanin. It's like a coloring.

So he makes more melanin than I do. I know we all have red blood, but when Mommy needed blood, the doctor said yours was different from hers.

That's right, there are several blood types: A, B, AB, and O. Group O is a universal donor. It has nothing to do with superiority or inferiority. Don't forget, it was Tam, your mother's Vietnamese friend, who gave blood to your mother, even though she is Moroccan. And yet they're from very different cultures and don't have the same skin color.

So if one day my friend Abdou needs blood, could I give him some of mine?

If you belong to the same blood group.

What's a racist?

A racist is someone who thinks he's better than other people just because his skin is a different color, or because he speaks a different language or celebrates certain holidays. A racist believes that there are several races and tells himself: "My race is the most beautiful and refined. The others are ugly and savage."

Is any race better than another?

No. Some writers in the eighteenth and nineteenth centuries tried to show that there was a white race that was physically and mentally superior to a supposed black race. At the time, humanity was thought to be divided into several races.

What are sociocultural differences?

Sociocultural differences are differences that distinguish one group from another by the ways in which people organize themselves in society (remember that each group has its own traditions and customs) and by what they create culturally. For example, African music is dif-

ferent from European music. Their cultures are different. The same is true of their marriage customs, holiday
rituals, and so on.

What are genetics?

"Genetics" refers to genes, the elements responsible
for the hereditary aspect of our existence. A gene is a
hereditary unit. Do you know what heredity is? It's
everything that parents transmit to their children, such
as physical and mental traits. Physical resemblances to
parents and certain character traits in children can be
explained by heredity.

Is education more responsible for our differences than genes?

We're all different from each other. But some of us share
hereditary traits. In general, people with the same traits
stick together. They form a population separated from
other groups by its way of life. There are several human
groups that differentiate among themselves by skin color,
by hair type, by facial features, and also by culture.

So if we're all different, then similarities don't exist.

Every human being is unique. No two human beings in the world are absolutely identical. Even twins are different. Each individual has an identity all his own. Each one is irreplaceable. Everyone can say: "I'm not like anyone else," and it's true. But to say, "I'm unique" doesn't imply "I'm better." It is simply noting that each human is unique; each being is a unique miracle.

Even me?

Absolutely. You're unique, just as Abdou is unique and Céline is unique. No two fingerprints in the world are the same. Each finger has its own imprint. That's why, in detective stories, detectives start by taking the fingerprints to figure out who was at the scene of the crime.

But daddy, on TV I saw a sheep that had been copied!

You're talking about cloning, reproducing something as many times as you want. This is possible with objects. There are machines that reproduce the same object identically. But it shouldn't be done with animals, and certainly not with people.

You're right. I wouldn't want two Célines in my class. One is enough.

Do you realize that if someone could reproduce human beings the way we make photocopies, that person would control the world? He could decide to reproduce some people and eliminate others.

It's scary. Even when it comes to my best friend, I wouldn't want a copy!

And if we authorized cloning, dangerous men could use it to their advantage, to seize power and crush the weak. It's a good thing that human beings are unique and can't be reproduced identically. I'm not the same as my neighbor, nor my twin brother. We're all different from one another.

Racists are afraid of foreigners because they're ignorant and think that there are several races and that theirs is the best?

Yes, but that's not all. You're forgetting about violence and the desire to dominate others.

Racists are wrong.

Racists are convinced that the group they belong to—which may be defined by religion, location, language or all three—is superior to other groups.

Why do they feel superior?

They believe and they convince others that there are natural inequalities that are physical or cultural in nature, which gives them a feeling of superiority over others. Some use religion to justify their behavior or their feelings, claiming that their religion is the best for everyone and that those who don't follow it are wrong.

Are you saying that religions are racist?

No, it's not religions that are racist, it's what people make of them that can encourage racism. In 1095, Pope Urban II declared war against Muslims, who were considered infidels. Thousands of Christians headed east to massacre Arabs and Turks. That war, fought in God's name, was called the "crusades."

Between the eleventh and the fifteenth centuries, Christians from Spain expelled the Muslims, and then the Jews, in the name of religion. Some people use sacred books to justify their desire to proclaim themselves superior to others. Religious wars are quite common.

But you told me once that the Koran was against racism.

That's right, the Koran is opposed to racism, just like the Torah and the Bible; all sacred books are opposed to racism. The Koran says that men are equal before God and are different only in the intensity of their faith. The Torah says: "If a stranger visits you, don't harm him, he will be for you as one of your countrymen... and you will love him as you love yourself." The Bible stresses loving your neighbor, which is to say all human beings, your neighbor, your brother, or a foreigner. The New Testament says: "I command you to love one another," and "Love thy neighbor as thyself." All religions preach peace among men.

What if you don't believe in God?

If you don't have faith, religious people may look down on you. The most fanatical may even consider you an enemy.

The other day when some people were killed, the journalist on TV blamed Islam. Do you think he's racist?

No, he's not racist; he's ignorant and incompetent. The journalist was confusing religion and politics. Some politicians use Islam to fight their battles. They're called fundamentalists.

Are they racist?

Fundamentalists are fanatics. Fanatics think they're the only ones who know the truth. Fanaticism and religion often go hand in hand. Fundamentalists exist in most religions. They believe they're following divine inspiration. They're blind, passionate, and want to impose their beliefs on everyone else. They're dangerous, because they don't value the lives of others. They're ready to kill and even to die for their God; many of them are controlled by a leader. Yes, they're racist.

They're like the people who vote for Le Pen?

Le Pen heads a political party based on racism, that is, based on hating of foreigners, immigrants, Muslims, Jews, and so on.

It's the Hatred Party!

Yes. But it's possible that not everyone who votes for Le Pen is racist. I wonder about that. Otherwise that would make four million racists in France! That's a lot! They're being fooled, or else they don't want to see the truth. By voting for Le Pen, some people are expressing their confusion, but they're not choosing the best way to do it.

What can we do so people will stop being racist?

As General de Gaulle said, "That's a tall order!" Hatred is a lot easier to establish than love. It's easier to be mistrustful and not love anyone than to love someone you don't know. There's always a spontaneous tendency to reject people, the impulse we were talking about before.

What does it mean to reject people?

It means closing your doors and windows. If a foreigner knocks, you don't open your door. If he keeps knocking, you open it, but you don't invite him in. You let him know he'd better go away; you kick him out.

And that creates hatred?

There is a natural mistrust people feel toward one another, but hatred is far more serious, and deeper, because it includes its opposite, love.

I don't understand. What kind of love are you talking about?

I'm talking about self-love.

Are there people who don't love themselves?

If you don't love yourself, you can't love anyone. It's like an illness. It's a miserable condition. But racists are often so in love with themselves there's no room for others. Hence their egotism.

So the racist is someone who doesn't love anyone and is an egomaniac. He must be very unhappy. It's hell!

Yes, racism is hell.

The other day, when you were talking to your brother, you said, "Hell is other people." What does that mean?

That has nothing to do with racism. It's an expression people use when they have to put up with people they don't want to deal with.

That's like racism.

No, not entirely, because you can't love everyone. If someone were to come into your room, tear up your notebooks, and prevent you from playing on your own, it wouldn't mean you were a racist if you kicked him out of your room. On the other hand, if your classmate—say Abdou, from Mali—came to your room and behaved himself and you kicked him out simply because he's black, then you'd be a racist. Do you understand?

Okay, but I still don't understand what you meant by "Hell is other people."

It's a phrase from a play by Jean-Paul Sartre called *No Exit.* After they die, three characters find themselves locked together in a room for eternity after their death. They have to live together; and they have no way out. That's hell. Hence the expression, "Hell is other people."

So that's not racism. I'm allowed not to love everyone. But how do you know when it's not racism?

You can't love everyone, and if you're forced to live with people you haven't chosen to live with, you might not like it and pick on them, which is what a racist does. To justify his disgust, however, a racist blames physical characteristics. He might say, "I can't stand so-and-so because he has a flat nose or because his hair is frizzy or his eyes are slanty." Deep down, racists think: "I'm not interested in knowing the strengths and weaknesses of a particular person. If he belongs to a certain group, I'll reject him." So he rejects someone based on physical or psychological traits.

Give me some examples.

Racists will say that blacks are "hearty but lazy, dirty and piggish." They'll say that the Chinese are "little, mean and selfish," that Arabs are "underhanded, aggressive traitors," that Turks are "strong and violent." Jews have been attributed the worst physical and moral defects to justify their persecution. There are lots of examples.

How do you fight it?

First, you have to learn respect. Respect is essential. People don't ask that you love them but that you respect their human dignity. Respect means being considerate. It's knowing how to listen. Foreigners don't expect love and friendship, but they require respect. Love and friendship can develop afterwards, when you get to know and appreciate someone. But in the beginning, nothing should be predetermined. In other words, you shouldn't have any prejudices. Racism develops out of preconceived notions about peoples and their cultures. All generalizations are stupid and lead us astray. That's why you should never say things like: "Arabs are this way or that way"; "The French are like this or that." Racists generalize based on an individual case. If an Arab robs them, they conclude that all Arabs are thieves. Respecting others means caring about justice.

So, basically, racism comes from 1) fear, 2) ignorance, and 3) stupidity?

That's right. But you should also be aware that someone could be very knowledgeable and use that knowledge to justify racism. Intelligence can be put to bad use. Sometimes even educated and cultivated people blame foreigners for their situation when something bad happens to them, like losing their job, for example. Deep down, they know that foreigners have nothing to do with it, but they need an outlet for their anger. In this case, the foreigner serves as a scapegoat.

What's a scapegoat?

Long ago, the Israelites picked a goat to which it symbolically attributed all its impurities, and left that goat in the desert. If you want to blame your own mistakes

on someone else, we say you are choosing a scapegoat.
In France, if there's an economic recession, racists
make people think it's because of the foreigners. They
accuse them of stealing jobs from the French, of stealing their bread and butter. The National Front, Le Pen's
racist party, put up posters all over France that said: "3
million unemployed = 3 million immigrants too many."
But do you know that one out of five Frenchmen is of
foreign origin!

**But immigrants also lose their jobs! Souad's
father, Mommy's cousin, hasn't worked
in two years. He keeps looking but can't find
anything. Sometimes he calls about a job
and they tell him he's hired, but when he
gets there they say it's too late!**
You're right. But racists are liars. They don't care about
the truth. What they want is to strike a chord with people by using slogans. Economic studies have shown that
the equation: "3 million unemployed = 3 million immigrants too many" is absolutely false. But someone who's

unhappy because he doesn't have a job is ready to believe anything to make himself feel better.

Accusing immigrants isn't going to help anyone find work!

Of course not. We're back to people's fear of foreigners, who are blamed for many problems and troubles. Racists are dishonest.

Dishonest?

I'll give you an example: a foreign student gets bad grades in school. Instead of blaming himself because he didn't study enough, he'll say he got bad grades because the teacher is racist.

That's like my cousin Nadia. She got a warning and she told her parents that the teachers didn't like Arabs! She's got a lot of nerve. I know it's because she's a bad student.

That's dishonesty!

But Nadia isn't racist.

She's using a weak argument to deny her own responsibility, and that's close to what racists do.

So we have to add dishonesty to the list, after fear, ignorance, and stupidity.

Yes. The reason I'm explaining to you how people become racist is because sometimes racism takes on tragic proportions. Then it's not just a matter of mistrust or jealousy. Throughout history, entire peoples have suffered at the hands of racism and extermination.

What's extermination? That sounds horrible.

It means completely and definitively doing away with a whole group or community.

How? By killing everyone?

That's what happened during the Second World War when Hitler, the leader of Nazi Germany, decided to eliminate Jews and Gypsies. He managed to gas and incinerate five million Jews.[*] That's called genocide. Underneath it all is a racist theory that says: "Jews are 'impure,' and therefore an inferior race. They have to be exterminated-eliminated down to the last person." In Europe, governments had to turn their Jewish citizens over to the Nazis. Jews had to wear yellow stars on their chests so they could be recognized. This kind of racism is called anti-Semitism.

Where does that expression come from?

It comes from the word "Semite," which refers to people who came from Western Asia and spoke similar languages, like Hebrew and Arabic. So Jews and Arabs are called Semites.

So if you're an anti-Semite, are you also anti-Arab?

In general, when we talk about anti-Semitism, we're talking about racism against Jews. This is a particular kind of

---

[*] This allusion to the five million Jews killed in the concentration camps and in the gas chambers by the Nazis comes from American historian Raoul Hilberg's book, *The Destruction of the Jews in Europe* (Fayard, 1988).

racism, since the killing of all the Jews was thought out
and planned in cold blood. But, to answer your question,
I would say racists don't like people who are different,
whether they're Jewish, Arabic or black. If Hitler had
won the war, he would have had to exterminate almost all
of humanity, because there is no such thing as a pure
race. It's nonsense. It's impossible. That's why we need to
be extremely vigilant.

Can Jews be racist?

Jews can be racist, just like Arabs, Armenians, Gypsies,
or blacks. There is no human group that doesn't have
individuals with racist feelings and behavior.

Even when you're a victim of racism?

Suffering injustice doesn't make you just. The same is
true for racism. A person who has been the victim of
racism can still be racist.

Tell me what genocide is.

Genocide is the systematic and methodical destruction
of an entire ethnic group. Someone powerful and crazy

decides to do whatever it takes to kill everyone belonging to a given group. In general, minority ethnic groups are the targets.

That's another word I don't know. What's an ethnic group?

It's a group of individuals with a common language, civilization, and customs transmitted from generation to generation. It's a people with a cohesive identity. The people in the group may live in different countries.

Give me some examples.

Jews, Berbers, Armenians, Gypsies, Chaldaens (people who speak Aramaic, the language of Christ). . .

If your group is small, could it be the victim of genocide?

History shows that minorities—peoples who exist in small numbers compared to the rest of the population—have often been persecuted. For instance, in this century, from 1915 on, the Armenians, who lived in the eastern provinces of Anatolia, were massacred by the Turks. More than a million people died out of a total population of 1,800,000. Then Jews were massacred in Russia and in Poland (those massacres were called pogroms). Right after that, the Nazis in Europe killed over five million Jews in concentration camps. From 1933 on, the Germans considered the Jews a "negative race," a "sub-race"; they also declared the Gypsies "racially inferior" and massacred them as well.

That was a long time ago. What about now?

Minority massacres continue. Recently, in 1995, the Serbs, in the name of what they called "ethnic cleansing," massacred thousands of Bosnian Muslims. In Rwanda, the Hutus massacred the Tutsis (a minority that was favored by the Europeans). These two ethnic groups have been at war ever since the Belgians colonized the Great Lakes region of Rwanda. Colonialism, which we'll talk about later, often divided populations in order to rule. This century has had its share of massacres and suffering. Slavery has been abolished just about everywhere in the world, but it still exists, disguised in many forms.

I've seen slaves in American movies.

Black Americans are descendants of slaves, seized chattel brought over from Africa. Slavery means owning a human being. The slave is totally deprived of freedom. He "belongs" to the person who buys him. Racism against blacks was and continues to be deeply rooted in America. Blacks fought hard for civil rights. Before, in certain states, blacks couldn't swim in the same pool as whites, couldn't use the same bathrooms, couldn't be buried in the same cemetery, couldn't ride in the front of a bus or attend the same schools. In 1957, in Little Rock, Arkansas, President Eisenhower, the police, and the army had to intervene so that nine black children could enter Central High School, a "white" school. The struggle for civil rights hasn't ended, despite the assassination, in 1968 in Memphis, of one of the great leaders of the struggle, Dr. Martin Luther King, Jr. Today, things are beginning to change. In South Africa, too, white and blacks once lived separately under a system called apartheid. The white minority that ruled the country discriminated against blacks, who were in the majority.

You said earlier than colonialism divided people. What's colonialism? Is it racism?

In the nineteenth century, European countries such as France, England, Belgium, Italy, and Portugal militarily occupied African and Asian countries. Colonialism is a form of domination. Colonists considered it their duty, as white, "civilized" people, to bring "civilization" to the "inferior races." They thought that Africans, because of their black skin, had less intellectual aptitude than whites; in other words, they weren't as smart as whites.

Colonists are racists!

They are racist and dominating. When you're ruled by another country, you're not free; you lose your independence. That's why Algeria, until 1962, was considered part of France. Its resources were exploited and its inhabitants weren't free. The French went to Algeria in 1830 and took over the entire country. Those who resisted were hunted down, arrested and killed. Colonialism is racism on a state level.

How can a country be racist?

Not an entire country, but if the government of a certain country arbitrarily decides to establish itself in lands that don't belong to it and to maintain itself by force, it must mean that it has contempt for the inhabitants of that land. It must consider the other culture worthless and in need of what it calls civilization. The colonizing government usually develops the country a little. It builds roads, schools, and hospitals, sometimes to show that it hasn't come solely for profit, yet the development is always to the colonizer's advantage. The colonizer develops what will help him best exploit the resources of the country. That's colonialism. Usually it's to acquire new wealth and increase power, but no one ever says that. It's an invasion, a theft, a brutalization with serious consequences. In Algeria, it took years of struggle, resistance, and war to end colonialism.

Were immigrants considered French before?

It was only after 1958 that people who came to France from Algeria were considered French, but not those from

Morocco or Tunisia. Others came on their own, like the Portuguese, the Spanish, the Italians, the Polish.

France is like America!

Not exactly. Many Americans are former immigrants, except for the Indians, who were the first inhabitants of the continent, and African Americans, who as slaves were forced immigrants. The Indians were massacred by the Spanish and then by the white Americans. When Christopher Columbus discovered the New World, he found Indians. He was surprised to realize that they were human beings, like Europeans, because at the time, in the fifteenth century, Europeans didn't believe Indians had souls. They were thought to be closer to animals than to human beings.

America is made up of several ethnic groups, of several populations from all over the world, whereas France became a land of immigrants only towards the end of the nineteenth century.

But, before the arrival of immigrants, was there racism in France?

Racism exists wherever people live. No country can claim to be free of racism. Racism is part of human history. It's better to know about it and learn to fight it. You have to watch yourself and think: "If I'm afraid of foreigners, they must be afraid of me." We're always a foreigner to someone. Learning to live together is how we fight racism.

But I don't want to learn to live with Céline. She's mean, she's a thief and a liar...

You're exaggerating!

She was mean to Abdou. She doesn't want to sit next to him in class, and she says mean things about black people.

Céline's parents obviously haven't taught her properly. Maybe they never learned themselves. But you shouldn't treat her the way she treats Abdou. You have to talk to her, explain to her why she's wrong.

I can't do that myself.

Then ask your teacher to discuss the problem in class.

You know, it's easier to change a child's behavior than a grown-up's.

Why, Daddy?

Because children aren't born with racists ideas. Usually a child repeats what his parents or relatives say. Children play naturally and freely with other children. They don't think about whether a child who's a different color is inferior or superior. For them, it's a playmate. Either they get along or they fight. That's normal. It has nothing to do with skin color. On the other hand, if your parents put you on guard against children of color, you'd behave differently.

But, Daddy, you keep saying that racism is common and widespread. That it's a human defect.

That's true, but a child has to be filled with healthy ideas so as not to give in to instinct. He can also be filled with false and unhealthy ideas. It depends a lot on your education and your parents' attitudes. Children should correct their parents when they say racist things. They shouldn't be intimidated by grown-ups.

What do you mean? That children can be saved from racism, but not adults?

Not so easily, that's right. Grown-ups have a hard time changing. Spinoza, a philosopher, said long ago: "Every being tends to persist in its being." A more common way of saying it is: "A zebra doesn't change its stripes." In other words, once you're grown, you are who you are. On the other hand, a child is still open to learning and being shaped. An adult who believes in the inequality of races is difficult to convince. Children, on the other hand, can change. That's what school is for, to teach them that men are born and remain equal, even if they're different from one another; and to teach them that human diversity is a source of wealth, not weakness.

Can racists be cured?

So you think racism is a disease?

Sure. It's not normal to reject someone because of his or her skin color...

The "cure" depends on them. On whether they are capable of self reflection.

What do you mean by that?

You need to ask yourself questions, to say to yourself: "Maybe I'm wrong to think the way I do." You make a concerted effort to change the way you think and act.

But you told me that people don't change.

Yes, but you can become aware of your faults and try to overcome them. It doesn't mean that you change completely. You adapt. Sometimes, when you're a victim of racism yourself, you realize how unfair and unacceptable it is. All you have to do is travel, to discover others, in order to realize it. Travel shapes young people. Traveling encourages a love of discovery and of learning. It means realizing the extent to which different cultures are rich and beautiful. No one culture is better than any other.

So there's hope...

You have to fight racism, because racists are dangerous and victims at the same time.

How can they be both at once?

They're dangerous to others and victims to themselves. They're wrong and they don't know it, or don't want to know it. It takes courage to recognize your mistakes. Racists don't have that courage. It isn't easy to recognize that you're wrong, to criticize yourself.

What you're saying isn't very clear.

You're right. I should be clearer. It's easy to say "you're wrong and I'm right." It's difficult to say "you were right and I was wrong."

I wonder if racists know they're wrong.

Well, they could know if they wanted to take the trouble, and if they had the courage to ask themselves some hard questions.

What kind of questions?

Am I really better than other people? Do I belong to a group that is superior to others? Are there groups that are "inferior" to mine? Even if there were inferior groups, why would I want to fight with them? Can a physical difference imply a difference in one's aptitude for knowledge? In other words, does having white skin really make you more intelligent?

What about weak people, sick people, old people, disabled people, children... are they inferior?

Only in the eyes of cowards.

Do racists know they're cowards?

No, because it takes courage to recognize one's cowardice.

Daddy, you're going in circles.

That's right, because I want to show you how the racist is a prisoner of his contradictions and can't escape them.

So it is a disease.

In a sense. When you escape, you move towards freedom. Racists don't like freedom. They're afraid of it. Just as they're afraid of differences. The only freedom they like is their own, the freedom that allows them to do whatever they like, to judge others and to hold them in contempt simply because they're different.

CONCLUSION

WE MUST DO WHAT WE CAN to fight against racism
every single day. We cannot allow ourselves to become
complacent. We can begin by setting a good example for
others; always paying attention to the words we use.
Words can be dangerous. They can be used to hurt and
humiliate people, to create hatred and mistrust. We have
to let go of preconceived ideas, to get rid of certain say-
ings and proverbs that are generalizations and may be
racist. The fight against racism begins with language.
This fight requires strength, perseverance, and imagination. It's not enough to take offense at racist language or
behavior. We have to speak up, never allowing a racist
remark to pass. Never say: "Oh, it doesn't matter!" If we
allow people to say or do bad things, we allow racism to
flourish even among people who might have avoided
falling into this trap. And by not acting or reacting, we
allow racism to become common and respectable. There
are actually laws in France regulating against racist
behavior. There are also associations and movements
that fight against all forms of racism.

When you go back to school, look at all the students. Notice how different they all are, how wonderful this diversity is. These students all come from different worlds. The mix is good for everyone.

Every face is unique, a miracle. No two faces are identical. Every face symbolizes a life and every life deserves respect. No one has the right to humiliate another human being. Everyone has the right to dignity. By respecting others, we honor life in all its beauty, magic, diversity and unpredictability. Respecting others allows us to respect ourselves.

POSTSCRIPT

Between January and May 1998, I visited fifteen secondary schools in France and Italy. Most of the students I met with were in seventh or eighth grade and had read Racism Explained to My Daughter.

They were not only interested in, but worried about racism. Those who seemed most concerned were the children of North African immigrants. Certain themes emerged from our discussions: questions of how to fight racism, how to integrate successfully, how to react to right-wing militancy and what the limits of tolerance should be.

The students were prepared for our discussions by their teachers. The book was explained, critiqued, and discussed. When I arrived, the students asked me questions they had previously tried out on their parents or instructors.

SARAH, eleven, with big, dark eyes, is a seventh grader at Clemenceau School in Montpellier. "What do you think of Arab parents who pull their kids out of a French school because it has too many Arabs?" she asked me. I asked her to repeat her question to determine whether she really meant Arab parents. "Yes," she told me. I expressed surprise, but then I thought to myself, "how can you explain self-hatred to a child?' I gave up and focused instead on the strong urge for assimilation. "Parents like that are eager for their child to be like the others, to be like French children," I said. "They think that by separating their child from other Arab children they can protect him or her from discrimination."

"But the child didn't want to change schools," Sarah interrupted, "Her parents are racist." Her teacher, who was at the meeting, explained, "She's talking about her own painful experience."

Of all the questions children asked me, Sarah's was the most unexpected and poignant. I was similarly disarmed by parents who confessed to feeling confused and helpless when they discovered that their children held racist beliefs or had even joined the National Front. These parents would say, shocked, "But we brought them up right!" or cite their membership in antiracist groups. At a bookstore in Paris, a mother confided that she and her husband were in the middle of a real crisis. "Our sons, fifteen and seventeen, are frequently attacked by North African boys," she said. "Whenever it happens I try to explain that they shouldn't generalize, but they're developing racist beliefs. What can we do? Your book doesn't deal with this problem."

The same issue was raised in other terms by a student from Bourges. "I have a hard time reasoning with my father," he explained. "He can't stand North Africans because they always park in front of our garage, which bugs him."

A teacher from Reims complained, "North African students speak Arabic to each other so that I can't understand. It's annoying. What can I do?"

Camille, fourteen, is a tenth grader at the same school. "How tolerant should people be? How am I supposed to react when our neighbor makes his fourteen-year-old daughter get married and wear a veil?"

Malika answered the question this way: "In France you can't do that. If my father made me get married I'd run away and stay with my best friend."

Khadija is a school administrator in Bourges. She

interrupted the students' discussion to ask me, "When are you going to write *Racism Explained to* My *Parents?*" She went on to describe her difficulty in getting her parents to accept her marriage to a non-Muslim. "To me, that's racism," she declared. "My parents are afraid of foreigners. I don't want the man I love to convert to Islam hypocritically just so my parents will accept him."

Houria is a twelve-year-old seventh grader in the Sévigné School in Roubaix. "Do you think you can influence a kid whose parents are racist?" he asked. Lydie, twelve, at the Jean Jaurès School in Lomme asked the same question. "If my family is racist, does that mean I am, too? Can I change them?" Her friend Karine chimed in, "At school we know a kid who's racist. He wouldn't read the book," she explained. "But it's not his fault; his family is strange. We tried to talk to him about it but couldn't get anywhere. We don't know what to do but we were hoping you could give us some good arguments."

Myriam is an eleventh grader at the Anatole de Monzie School in Bazas. Born in France of Algerian parents, she explains that her older brother in Toulon had to change his first and last names "so he could find a job and have a normal life." She paused, then added, "It didn't help, because he couldn't change his face. On the other hand, I feel pretty comfortable here."

Malek is a child of French and Algerian parents. "I learned to use humor to deal with racism," he says. "When we lived in Bordeaux, I would laugh off racist remarks, but my sister was really bothered by them. Now she has problems and has to go to a shrink."

Not all young people have the ability to laugh off racist remarks. Wherever I went I was asked the same question: "How should I react when confronted by racist aggression? You don't say in the book what to do when that happens."

That's true; the book doesn't address this. I would say, however, that it is important to react and not let racial slurs slide by. Do not fool yourself into believing that there is such a thing as a mild form of racism any more than there are recreational drugs. Light beer and diet soft drinks, maybe; "racism light," no. There are laws against inciting racial hatred. One day, during a discussion at the Alain Borne School in Montélimar, the headmaster began signaling me. A teacher whispered in my ear. "Be careful not to encourage violence in school," he said. "It's a serious problem here. We don't want students to think it's okay to fight." I clarified my position by noting that one should never respond to one slur with another, but instead stay calm and take advantage of the opportunity to talk about different views together as a class.

Audrey, an eighth grader at the same school, told me that she had never been subjected to racism and had never been racist herself. "The North Africans who live in France are racist toward the French," she complained. "Some of the foreigners living in France don't obey our laws." Laurent, a member of the same class, took the same tack. "Racism is mostly caused by blacks and North Africans toward whites," he declared. "When a French person kills an Arab, it gets talked about for two weeks on the news, but when it's the other way around, people forget about it after two or three days." Another student passed me a note saying "I'm not racist, but there are some Arabs I don't like because they're jerks. I've really been dumped on by Arabs." Marion: "Whether we're blue, green, black, red, yellow, or white, we all have a heart and a brain. I've never been racially insulted, and I don't believe I've ever insulted anyone." Echoing Marion's feeling, Léa, a twelfth grader in the Anatole de Monzie School in Bazas, told me that she had a confession to make. "When I was little I called a friend a 'nigger'; I never did it again, though."

Jessica, twelve, an eighth grader in Reims, asked, "If your parents and friends aren't racist, how do you become one yourself?" Her classmate, Arthur, wondered, "How would you react if you found out your daughter was a racist?" Marion asked, "Has your daughter ever been a victim of racism?" Frédéric followed with: "Have you ever been a direct victim of racism?"

I surprised them by saying that neither I nor my children had been victims of racism, at least not in a direct or violent form. This led some North African students to observe that we were "privileged."

Before making this trip around France, I had no idea that young people ages eleven to fifteen years old could be so concerned about the National Front. They equate the party with racist crimes and do not understand why democratic France allows the movement to keep growing. Every question asked by the tenth-grade classes at the school in Montpellier had to do with the danger of the National Front. In Reims, Hicham, 14, said to me, "If one day the French Republic ceased to exist and an anti-immigrant dictator took over, how would you react?" When I asked him to elaborate, he added: "The National Front wants to set up a dictatorship and get rid of the Republic. That's their goal, and they'll do whatever they say they're going to do."

Another North African student asked, "If there are laws against racism, how come a party like the National Front isn't banned?" Rachid, from the school in Montpellier, put it another way, "How tolerant do you have to be? Does tolerance apply to everybody all the time?"

At that point I couldn't resist praising intolerance when justice and people's dignity are at risk. Injustice, humiliation, and murderous hatred must not be tolerated. Tolerance is a virtue as long as it doesn't turn into passivity in the face of things that should not be tolerated. It is important to be tolerant and to respect differences, but it is equally important to continue to draw distinctions and to be vigilant. There is no room for tolerance when faced with militant, vengeful, and cruel racism. At that point, you have to defend yourself. Sometimes it's a matter of defending yourself from bodily harm, of saving your life and your children's lives.

Constance, a student in the same class, asked me how I felt about the growth of the National Front. Noémie wanted to know "In a country that promotes human rights, how can a party like the National Front be allowed to exist?"

Most of the students in Bazas are from the countryside. A teacher told me that "racism is practically unknown here." At the end of our meeting the children told me that were it not for the book they would not have known that racial hatred existed. In the whole school I saw just one student with black skin and one North African. Myriam, the North African, was totally assimilated and spoke with the local accent. No foreign-

ers, no racism? Don't be so sure. In talking with the children I realized that the question of racism bothered
them, even if it was not a central concern. Aurélie asked
me, "Can you be racist without knowing it?" Elodie
wanted to know what drove me to publicly condemn
racism. The only black child in the school said nothing.
As I was leaving, though, he came up to me shyly and
held out the book so I could sign it. "Sir," he said,
"what's the point of racism?"

Estelle, an eighth grader in a school in Reims asked,
"Did you weigh the pros and cons before writing this
book?" Aurélie, a member of the same class, wanted to
know if I had ever succeeded in converting a racist.

Other themes and lines of questioning entered into
the discussions. North African children in particular spoke
frequently of fear, not of racial violence but of not finding
a place in French society. Hanane, fourteen, asked me to
define integration. What she wanted to know was whether
she, who had been born in France of Algerian parents and
spoke Arabic at home, would one day be integrated. Her
question echoed Sarah's query about Arab parents who

did not want their children mixing with Arabs and reminded me of Myriam's brother, who had changed his name to fit in. So many children of immigrants have become average French kids and have difficulty imagining a life in their parents' country of origin. They are the ones who show the most concern about racism. In clear and simple language, they proclaim their desire not to be excluded from this country and its history.

The children of Bazas, the ones who said they had never experienced racism, asked a question in unison. "How would you like to see us grow up?" Thomas, an eighth grader in Montélimar, handed me a piece of paper on which he had scrawled, "Racism is like having your eyes at war with each other." On another page he wrote this confession: "I can't understand the stupidity of racists. They're not very smart. I'm against racism because I know that all the races are equal. White, black, or yellow; they're the same. Since I was little I've had different kinds of friends."

It is April 9, 1998, and I am meeting with primary- and middle-school students in the auditorium of the city hall in Rome. The children, ages ten to fourteen, are accompanied by their teachers, and in some cases by their parents.

"According to your book," says Roberto, twelve, "racism is more widespread among whites than among blacks, but it also exists among blacks. What can we do to stop it in both groups?" I remind him that people of color have always been the victims of slavery. Yet this has not stopped the victims of discrimination from being unjust to people different from themselves.

Isabelle, thirteen, arrived in Italy from Ethiopia when she was five. "How do you explain the fact that some people still believe in fascism after all that has happened?"

Dalac, twelve, an Ethiopian girl, asked, "In addition to fear and ignorance, what feelings or traits contribute to racism?"

I want to answer: stupidity.

Michele, thirteen, broke in, "If racism comes from ignorance, why are smart and educated people some-times racist?"

Culture—knowledge, awareness, education—does not always coincide with ideas of goodness and progress. It is possible to know a lot about other people and still to behave as if one were superior to them, to believe and to make others believe that one's own culture is better than another. And yet what characterizes cultures is their diversity and their differences, which imply no moral or political value judgments. I remember a slogan I heard during a demonstration against the National Front in Paris on March 28, 1998: "Intelligence stops where racism starts."

Fabio, thirteen, said, "Racism is like humidity. Over time, the house crumbles."

Sylvia, ten, asked, "Do you think man is free?"

What do you say to a child who asks such a serious question? I tell her that man's freedom is in his own hands. "If he decides to be free, he'll be free, in the sense that no one can stop his thoughts."

Guido, fifteen, is a student at the Vecchi de Trani science high school in Puglia. "I think the situation in Italy is as bad as it is in France," he says. "Here, we have something really sad: hatred for people from southern Italy. I don't think you can ever wipe out racism completely. I've had racist thoughts about homeless people who smell bad. What my reaction showed me was basically that I would do anything to prevent reaching that stage of degradation. It's preventive racism: I don't want to put myself in a situation in which I would be rejected by others."

I explained that the revulsion he felt was not really racism but a sort of discomfort or anxiety. In fact, it meant, by trying out racist feelings, he did not ever want to be in the position of being a victim of racist behavior.

Elisa, fourteen, is a student in the same school. She said to me, "It's easy to explain racism to your daughter, who's not a racist. How do you explain it to someone who is intolerant or openly racist?"

Intolerance and racism necessarily imply a form of behavior that excludes dialogue. So how do you talk to someone who refuses to listen, who does not want to believe you, and who clings desperately to his or her positions? I would say that you have to answer arrogant racists with the law. The three white Texans who attacked a black man on June 10, 1998, and who dragged him behind their car until he died are not going to listen to reason. They'll understand nothing but the penalties of justice.

Giovanni, thirteen, chimed in. "So how do you explain racism to a child whose parents are racist?"

A special class of the Capitaine Lagache School in Paris's twentieth arrondissement is composed of students whose grades were not good enough to allow them to enter seventh grade. They are being prepared for a different kind of education. Some will go back to middle school, some to technical schools, and some will drop out, unable to escape the stigma of academic failure. The pupils are between twelve and fourteen. Most are from poor immigrant families. To be in such a class has a twofold meaning for them: it is a sign of their failure in school and means that their future prospects will be increasingly limited. They are aware of all this and discuss it openly and clearly, although there is despair, too, in their voices. Racism is experienced here as the consequence of the exclusion that lies ahead for them, because they know that these special classes are often nothing more than waiting rooms from which there is nowhere to go but the street.

The teachers do what they can. They are commendable, not only for their teaching but also for giving hope and courage to adolescents who see that society is unable to save them and integrate them. So they turn to others and make remarks tinged with racism, anger, and despair.

Kader, fourteen, was born in France of Algerian parents. He is the most talkative member of the class, and the most anxious. He wonders why Arabs and Muslims should be badly dressed, be sweeping streets, and have dirty hands from doing manual labor while "the Jews wear spotless clothes and give orders in offices, banks, and hospitals. I would like to know," says Kader, "why we always get bad grades and why we're always last."

"Why single out the Jews?" I ask him.

Kader pauses before telling me that "they don't like us."

Kader had read my book. He knew what the Jews had endured and how they had been persecuted. But he faulted me for not having pointed out that today they are "unfair and mean to Arabs." He was referring to the Israeli-Palestinian conflict.

His remark took me back once again to the question posed by Sarah, the seventh grader from the Clémenceau School in Montpellier, who had been hurt by being withdrawn from a school where her parents thought there were too many Arabs. Arabs are viewed unfavorably, and Arab children feel the effects in their own lives and in their relationships with others. This form of racism, founded on self-hatred, is reinforced by the pain of failure in school or in the job market. A child who perceives that he has no future in this society and in this country is psychologically brittle and lacks an anchor. Daily confrontations with others add salt to the wound. Failure in school is viewed as one more example of general rejection. Although, in principle, being economically disadvantaged might induce one to work harder, poverty produces inverse reactions in some cases, reactions born of defeat and resignation.

The public schools, secular and democratic in their ethos, are powerful engines for the integration of immigrants' children. To complete the process of integration, however, work needs to be done with families and their immediate surroundings. The media, in particular, plays an essential role in this daily struggle against poor self-image. If we don't take action, racism will push through society's cracks and fault lines and take root in people's minds as they try either to maintain their status or to compensate for a lack of insight and reasoning power.

FRENCH LEGAL PROVISIONS
DEALING WITH RACISM

A law passed unanimously by the French National Assembly on July 1, 1972, punishes racial slurs and defamation as well as "incitements to hate or violence toward a person or group of persons on account of their origin or their membership or nonmembership in a given ethnicity, race, or religion."

The same law permits antiracist associations that have existed for at least five years to file civil actions.

On December 9, 1948, the United Nations accepted genocide as a crime against humanity and defined it as an indefeasible crime committed with the intent to destroy, in whole or in part, a national, ethnic, racial, or religious group. As soon as an act of genocide is identified, member states are expected to intervene to prevent or to punish it.

Patricia Williams and her son Ross

Racism Explained to My Son

PATRICIA J. WILLIAMS

I DISCOVERED Tahar Ben Jelloun's *Racism Explained to my Daughter* when I was in France with my five year old. Knowing my interest in the complexities of prejudice, a friend pushed the book into my hand as a departure gift as I rushed through a Paris train station on my way to visit other friends, a British family who had a house in the lushly picturesque region of the Dordogne.

It was an odd summer. My son and I ended up staying in a little enclave of stables turned into vacation houses leased mostly by staunch denizens of Middle England who, with the exception of my friends, tended to look upon their rural French neighbors as "charming, apple-cheeked peasants." [Our French neighbors tended to derogate the British in terms colorful enough to gravely imperil that reputation for charm.] Add in a couple of black Americans and one could not find a more perfect setting from which to contemplate the forces of race, class, language, and nationality as they swirled in an eddy of tribute to the new globalism.

It is always a challenge living away from what one knows best, but this was a summer in which all the challenges came from unexpected sources. I had expected to feel American first and foremost, but these particular good French citizens merely puffed their cheeks at my American-ness and sighed with relief that at least I was Not British.

Then came the matter of language. I had expected to feel anxiety about my French, which while good is shy and formal, but my French friends dubbed it "amazingly good for an American." In fact, it was so good that sometimes I was mistaken for an "immigrant," which is, I assure you, not nearly as much fun as being a tourist. Rather than not sounding French enough, the bigger problem, particularly for my son, was not sounding English enough. While the French laughingly encouraged his faltering forays into their language, the Brits were far less tolerant of his fluent Americanisms. When thirsty, he would ask for "whaw-tturr," in his very standard middle-class American accent. "Woe-tah," the British children would correct, as their mothers would worry aloud about my son's influence. "Of course you can't help the way you speak," said one. "It's just that learning down is so much easier than learning up," said another.

As for race, to the French my brown skin was the source of some occasional, low-level anti-immigrant sentiment until it was discovered I was from the United States, at which point brown became black, became exotic, fantastical. "Are you from the Bronx?" asked the woman who sold me my daily *Herald Tribune*, as though daring to dream. Her voice was filled with such glad anticipation that I almost hated to disappoint her.

Explaining any of this to my son was a complicated matter. To me, as an adult (and no doubt as a tourist), anti-immigrant prejudice in France has a more diffusely condescending, colonialist feel than the direct, competitive backlashing anger of racism and xenophobia in the United States. To my son, it just hurt his feelings.

To me, British class bias is a great albatross upon their necks alone; some precious degree of their life's creativity is utterly sapped by the contortions of eternal social climbing and angst about accent. Personally, I was relieved to be mostly on the outside of their microscopic and needlessly cruel assessments of one another. But to my son it just felt like exclusion.

To all the children of this complicated summer, however, it was our romanticized African-Americanness that was the object of greatest confusion and interrogation. "Have you ever been beaten?" asked one little French girl who had read all about Martin Luther King and little else. "But you're not black," protested a British pre-schooler, meaning that I was light brown. I tried to explain that race was a political designation—but then got quite tangled up trying to explain "political" to an almost five year old. And then: "I know Michael Jordan," volunteered my intrepidly fanciful son, who knows nothing if not how to milk a moment. And his little companions, every last gullible one of whom had seen *Space Jam* and in a variety of languages, not only believed him, but thenceforth delivered him a degree of respect that had eluded him when we were mere "slave stock" (as the British tabloid,

The Daily Mail, had referred to me only a few months before in announcing a BBC lecture I was giving).

It was against this backdrop, amid the exhaustion of perpetual explanation, that I began idly reading Ben Jelloun's slender volume, to myself at first, then aloud to my son. It was such a lucid, elegantly written little handbook, perfectly calibrated for young ears. Children—even, or should I say particularly, very young ones like my son—are hungry for some logic to explain the irrationalities of being marked and mocked. Their questions are too often greeted with deflections, silence, or sunny, universalizing coverups. Too many adults, I think, diminish the significance of playground racism by denying the degree to which little ones have already absorbed, like sponges, some very unbecoming attitudes from the world around them.

The lucidity of *Racism Explained to My* **Daughter** makes it as useful for adults as for the young. It provides the simplest of entrées into a subject that, with increasing age, tends to become increasingly emotionally laden for most people. Many adults have difficulty deciphering the complexities of prejudice for themselves, never mind for their children. It is, indeed, clearly a book intended to be read by parents to and with their children. Even now that I am back in the United States, sitting at home reading this English translation to myself, I can still hear my son's voice mingling with the questions asked by Ben Jelloun's daughter. I can still remember how startled I was by some of the issues he posed; how surprised I was at what he had tried to resolve by himself—and might never have discussed with me were it not for the gentle invitation of this book.

Yet, when I use words like lucid, I do not want to leave the impression that this is a book without nuance. It is precisely the horrendous complexities of racism's various and intertwined histories that make it imperative that we provide explanations at many levels, and for many different audiences. I daresay that there will be some Americans who will find this book a help (in that it offers an encompassingly international perspective on prejudice) but also a hindrance (in that it does not deal specifically with the kind of passionate violence and interpersonal taboo that so often permeate the racial confrontations to which even children are exposed in the United States).

My enthusiasm for this book stems from the fact that I can think of so few books—perhaps Langston Hughes's poems and essays for young people?—that have provided any starting point nearly this thoughtful; this book helps fill a void. And for the children of our rapidly changing world, I think that it is unequivocally helpful to have a high-minded reference, albeit general, that allows them to acknowledge both contemporary and historical systems of bias, yet which leaves room for them to imagine and create worlds beyond. Ben Jelloun writes in a way that fixes neither blame nor responsibility in any rigid way, but fully allows for the malleability of prejudice. It makes no one heroic in the battle against bias, but makes clear how seductive are the stories all people tell themselves when indulging sly mixtures of innocence and hate.

As this world grows increasingly diasporic, the traumas of the past and evolving present will re-present themselves to us and to our children in new disguises, new hybrids, and new junctures. Racism, anti-Semitism, xenophobia, class prejudice, and whatever else there will be in this world to hate are often represented as thorns and thistles in our planetary Garden of Eden. Tahar Ben Jelloun's great contribution is to remind those still open enough to hear it, that hate cannot always be divined by those who are looking only for weeds. He reminds us that that which is most insidious in life often resembles a beautiful blossom, a ripe fruit of one's culture, a consensus of one's trusted peers, an attitude purveyed by those intimates one loves and trusts the most. Ultimately, what I love best about this little book is that Ben Jelloun's explanation to his daughter does not end with the last page, but in its simple, subtle fashion, leaves readers young and old positioned squarely on the doorstep of lifelong moral inquiry, in which the self is never exempt.

David Mura with his daughter Samantha Sencer-Mura.

Explaining Racism to my Daughter

DAVID MURA

This happened last year:

I AM PUTTING my daughter to bed. She's eight, in third grade, a child of a Japanese American father and a mother who is three-quarters WASP and one-quarter Austrian Hungarian Jewish. I'm asking Samantha about her new friends at school, her classmates. Among other things I inquire about their ethnic and racial backgrounds, about whether these matters affect the relationships in her class.

Samantha says she really doesn't think about such things. Certainly most of her friends don't think about them as much as she does.

She says she thinks my asking about whether people are Asian American or African American or white, is racist. She tells me racism is something from the old days, like the internment camps or segregation. It doesn't really affect her life.

She implies that we should be beyond thinking about people in groups.

My daughter's words here don't reflect all her views on this subject. She's contradicting herself (as we all do). I know she was bothered when people mistook her in second grade for another Asian American girl or when her classmates implied she had a connection to this girl simply because of their Asian faces. I know she's played the role of Confucius in a skit before her class—a role she chose—and when she performed she told them pointedly that "Confucius is not from my country." I know we've talked about the media presentations of Asians and Asian Americans, of the stereotypes that still permeate present day American media. Once, in first grade, she and her friend Diwa, a Filipino Thai American, proclaimed that since Disney was not producing any feature films about Asian Americans they were going to make their own Asian American video (this was before *Mulan*). When Samantha and Diwa were even younger and were watching the old Disney *Peter Pan* they both turned to each other and said, "My mother says that Native Americans are really not like this."

None of this, though, comes up in her mind in our conversation in the dark of her bedroom just before sleep.

In a way, my daughter is telling me that my preoccupation with race is itself racist. That I should move beyond worrying about these matters. That we should just deal with people as people, not as Asian American or African American or white or Bosnian or Tibetan or Swedish American.

What should I tell her? Do her words indicate I need to teach her a new and more complicated way of thinking about racism? Or do they indicate some generational shift, some way of perceiving the subject that she and her generation feel and I do not? Or is it both?

When my daughter calls me a racist, how should I respond?

WE ARE TOLD that certain Inuit tribes use two dozen words referring to the snow. The implication is that such precision is required for the survival of the tribe. They need to be able to pinpoint these features of their environment, the shifts in the weather. One word is simply not an adequate set of tools.

We can see that racism threatens both children of color and white children in America, though in different ways. We know that it forms a crucial part of the environment they must grow up in and live with. We know it affects many aspects of their lives—where they will live, whom they go to school with, how they will be educated, whom they will become friends with, whom they fall in love with, whom they will work with and for, where they will work, what their salaries will be. It may even, as certain statistics indicate, help determine their health and how long they will live.

And yet we have only one word to approach this subject with: Racism.

Perhaps because he is a writer, Tahar Ben Jelloun realizes that understanding racism involves a construction of language; racism possesses its own dictionary. His dialogue with his daughter is filled with painstaking definitions. It starts with the overall term racism. From this a whole and necessary vocabulary unfolds: *different, foreigner, prejudice, impulse, discrimination, ghetto, melanin, sociocultural differences, blood types, genetics, scapegoat, extermination, genocide, ethnic groups, slavery, apartheid, colonialism.* Some of these terms indicate practices or beliefs; some are scientific, some are political. Some, like ghetto or apartheid or slavery, require historical background and bring up questions about economics.

"What is racism?" a child asks. Perhaps only in the face of such a simple inquiry do we realize how difficult the answer is. It's rare, though, that we're asked such a pointed question about the subject. More often the subject appears obliquely or without an open invitation. A racist slur someone made at school, an old movie or cartoon on television with blatant and historic stereotypes, a racist opinion voiced at a family gathering, a politician with whom we agree or disagree, a demonstration on the news, an act of racial violence or hatred—we and our children confront such triggers to speak about racism in our daily lives. Some of us may use these occasions to speak to our children, some let them pass. But rarely do we go into as full and open discussion as Tahar Ben Jelloun undertakes here with his daughter.

The fact is that there few other such texts we can give to our children. This tells us something about the state of race relations in our culture and our present abilities and efforts to educate our children about this subject.

TO BE PRECISE, my daughter did not call me a racist. She said that my way of speaking and thinking about people was racist. This was because I seemed to pay inordinate attention to the grouping of people by race and ethnicity. The implication was that I should look at them as individuals and not as members of a group.

I suspect that my daughter might agree with Ben Jelloun when he says, "I suggest you stop using the word 'race.' It's been so exploited by bad people that it's better to replace it with the word humanity. The human species is composed of various groups. But all men and all women on this planet have the same color blood in their veins, whether their skin is pink, white, black, brown, yellow or anything else."

Certainly Ben Jelloun is correct when he states that "The word 'race' has no scientific basis. It was used to exaggerate the effects of outward, physical appearance." "Race" is a fictional concept, a social not a natural construct.

And yet this fictional concept affects how people think and behave in the world. In that sense it is neither unreal nor non-existent. It is a very powerful social force. And this means that although we are all one species, although we all have the same color blood in our veins, we do not act and think alike. We do not possess the same experiences.

For some people in American society, the categories of race have caused a whole range of negative experiences. For other people the same categories have enabled them to escape from these experiences. For some people the categories of race have excluded them from certain privileges. For others the same categories have availed them of certain privileges. For all people the categories of race have meant their ancestors experienced different histories.

We cannot speak of these differences in experience, privileges, and histories without referring to racial categories and the way they are used in our society.

Simply to stop speaking of such categories does not destroy or erase the social practices based on them. It does not erase the fact that unemployment among blacks in America has historically been twice that for whites. It does not erase the fact that the students in mainly white suburban Winnetka benefit from an education that costs thousands of dollars more than the students in the mainly black south side of Chicago. It does not erase the fact that it is far easier for a young white male than a young black male to receive a loan, or hail a city taxi, or drive through a suburban white neighborhood unmolested by the police. For this reason I would not tell my daughter, as Ben Jelloun does, to stop using the word "race." Perhaps it is a flawed or inadequate tool, a word which has been much misused, but without it, we are forced into silence. And the real causes and conditions of racism would be left untouched.

SO WHAT DO I DO with my daughter's reactions? I have told her that it's been my experience that many white people, even well intentioned ones, have difficulty understanding my own experiences as a person of color in America or my views on race. This is not as true with the people of color I meet.

She says that it seems then that I am prejudiced against white people. I am categorizing people by race.

I tell her that in one sense she's correct. I know there are white people with whom I can trust discussing my most inner feelings about race, but I also know there are fewer of them than people of color. Therefore I tend, at least initially, to trust people of color in some ways more than I do whites. It is a prejudice.

My daughter senses here a double standard. In this, her thinking is not very different from many conservative thinkers.

Take the case of a white person who believes people of color are more likely to be criminals or to bring down property values and who therefore does not want to live in neighborhoods with a majority of people of color. Statistically the white person may be correct. And what if the white person says that he or she would accept people of color who have good middle class values, who share their socioeconomic status and who act like them? This isn't really prejudice, many would say; it's just common sense. Of course, I believe such thinking is racist. But if this person is prejudiced, my daughter might ask, are they any more prejudiced than me, given my admission of a racially based sense of trust? My daughter wants to live in a world where people are not judged by the color of their skin. She wants to live in a world where the terms "racism" and "race" no longer exist. She believes that the way to accomplish this is not to pay attention or acknowledge differences in race. To do otherwise is to be prejudiced. This is the same argument many conservatives use against affirmation action. We should not, the argument goes, grant privileges or benefits to anyone because of their membership in a given race. This is discrimination.

Can I satisfactorily explain to my daughter that my distrust of white people is not the same as a white person's distrust of people of color? Can I explain to her the reasons behind affirmative action? That it is, in some cases, necessary and a good thing to group people by race in order to redress a social injustice? How am I to do this?

TO START OFF, I need to help my daughter see that we are both individuals and members of groups. The two facts are not mutually exclusive. That is, if you look at a person as a member of a group, this does not mean you cannot look at them as an individual. Indeed the opposite is true: Without knowing about the group the individual belongs to, how can adequately know who they are? The more you know about Asian Americans, their histories and cultures, the more you're able to realize that we are not all alike. It's only if you're ignorant of our background and our ethnic groups that this happens.

For a child, and perhaps for most of us, the difficult task here is to move beyond the limits of a focus on the individual. This is particularly hard for Americans to do, given our cultural and historical emphasis on the individual.

What does such a shift in perspective mean in talking about race with my daughter? I must enable her to see that the practice of racism in society involves more than the acts of deluded or frightened or insecure or hateful individuals. Instead racism is, at its base, a social, political and economic system which works on a group as well as an individual level. In other words my daughter must understand that individual acts of racism affect the workings of the society as a whole, and that these individual acts must be connected systematically. In doing this I must enable my daughter to see that racism is a system of power as well as of beliefs and actions. More specifically it is a system through which the power and resources of a given society are distributed unequally and unjustly. This system of power can be supported by silence and non-action as well as by active participation.

The system of power must also be supported by a system of beliefs. Some of these beliefs which support this system are recognized as racist. Others which support the system are not.

Needless to say, to explain all this is not an easy task. The concepts here are difficult for an adult to grasp much less a nine-year-old.

It is no wonder then that Ben Jelloun's dialogue with his daughter falls short in this. Part of the problem is that despite all his useful definitions and explanations he tends to address racism primarily as a moral and psychological or at times a historical issue.

But racism is also a political issue. Ben Jelloun, I feel, slights the view of racism as a system of power.

IN THE PAST, white Americans used racial insults much more openly than they do now. Particularly after the civil rights movement in the 1950s and '60s such words became more and more taboo.

In 1999, in American public life, we believe those who use those racial insults to hurt others are racist. Most whites also believe what they regard as a simple corollary: If you know these terms are wrong and don't use them, then you are not racist. Such terms becomes a litmus test and are used by many whites to assuage their conscience, to assure themselves they are not racist.

In reality things are not so simple. For one thing there are those who know these words are wrong and still use them in situations where they think no one will criticize them. Often this takes place in private with other whites. People who listen to this use and say nothing do not necessarily believe they themselves are racist.

Indeed people who use these terms privately or even openly do not always think of themselves as racist. Marge Schott, the owner of the Cincinnati Reds baseball team, was caught speaking of some of her ball players as "million dollar niggers"; she used the terms "kike" and "Japs." Yet when she was confronted with evidence of her remarks, she replied that she was not a racist. Her mouth spoke these words and not her heart.

The truth is that any time someone is publicly accused of being a racist, that person will immediately get up and say they are not racist. Their friends will be interviewed and they will say that this person is not a racist, that he or she doesn't have a racist bone in his or her body. After all, to admit being friends with a racist is to appear to be racist oneself.

One reason for this behavior is that we have equated being racist with being evil. It is generally believed that those who are racists are particularly loathsome; the label associates them with historically recognized villains such as Hitler, slave owners, and the Ku Klux Klan. If people have the choice between admitting to being a racist and being evil and not being a racist and not being evil, most people will say that they are not racists.

Unfortunately the real state of race relations and the real presence of racism in our society is much more complicated than this. There are many more racists in our society than people who will admit to being racist. There are many more racists in our society than most white people will acknowledge. This silence, this denial, is the one of the ways racism is allowed to flourish.

FOR MANY WHITES, an exception such as Marge Schott only reinforces their sense of their own innocence. They regard racism as the acts of a few deluded individuals. One reason for this belief is their definition of racism. A large number see racism solely as the acts of individuals and do not believe that racism is systematically built into our society. In contrast many more people of color believe racism works systematically as well as through individuals. One reason for this discrepancy is that most whites believe that racial insults are the prime indicator and example of racism. The absence of these examples in their lives says to them

racism has vanished or is a great deal less prevalent
than in the past.

In contrast many people of color believe that racism
possesses many more forms of social practice than racial
insults. They realize this because these more complicated and less obvious forms of racist practice adversely
affect their lives.

It is easy to see that a white person calling someone
a "nigger" or a "gook" is a racist act. It is a lot harder to
see how the disparities in income in this country
between whites and African Americans are caused by
racism. It is easy to see a cross burning on someone's
lawn and to interpret it as a calling card for white
supremacy. It is much more difficult to see the ways
African Americans are consistently denied access to bank
loans in ways whites are not. Nor are such "invisible" acts
commonly regarded as supporting white supremacy. The
individual racist act is easy to witness and admit. The
workings of the racist system are not.

Successful African Americans understand the way
white Americans view the world. This does not mean

they agree with it but they must understand it to be successful. In contrast most successful white Americans do not understand the way African Americans view the world. One reason for this is that their success does not depend upon this knowledge. In fact in many ways their success depends on a ignorance of this knowledge. The difference in the situation of successfol African Americans and successful white Americans reveals something about who holds power in our society. Whom the structures and means of power are meant to benefit. Who is supposed to have an easier way.

To see the workings of this system means most whites must find a different way of interpreting and describing what they see. They must also find a way to see things they do not see. They must move out of the familiarities of their normal lives and vision. Richard Wright once remarked that black and white Americans are engaged in a battle over the description of reality. Why is this so? One obvious reason is that their experiences are different and so they interpret the facts of the world around them differently. Another is that the portion of the America experience that blacks see is generally quite different than that witnessed by whites: When they describe America, whites and people of color are often describing two different worlds.

ONE TALE ABOUT RACE I discuss with my daughter is the case of Texaco. In this corporate version of the Rodney King video, executives of Texaco were caught on audiotape discussing practices of racial discrimination in the company and ways of covering up those practices in face of a law suit. The existence of this tape produced a general public consensus: There were individuals who discriminated against African Americans at Texaco. Moreover this practice was so widespread it could be deemed as systematic within the company. And yet most discussions about Texaco did not truly examine how this system was allowed to flourish. People first focused on the open racial insults on the tape (whose context was revealed later to be somewhat ambiguous). They then focused on the admission that there was evidence that certain individuals did discriminate against African

Americans. Yet the existence of discrimination at Texaco did not simply depend upon these individuals who acted in an obvious racist manner. It also depended upon those who knew about these practices and did nothing to stop them. It also depended upon those who did not know about these practices.

You can be sure that the vast majority of African Americans at Texaco knew these practices existed. Those who did not know were mainly white. At the same time whites in the company benefited from these practices and received advances in an unequal and unjust manner. Are those who did not know of these practices innocent of racism? Are those who knew about them and were silent innocent? I would argue, No.

If they had said something about these practices, if they did the work needed to learn about these practices and protest them, then the racist system at Texaco could not have been implemented. The system *depended* upon their silence and ignorance.

You can view the case of Texaco as a microcosm of racism in the United States.

A vast majority of whites have chosen, consciously and unconsciously, to be silent about and to ignore racist practices of other whites or to be ignorant about such practices. At the same time they accept the benefits they receive as whites in this racist system. The system will not change until whites stop their silence and ignorance and stop their acceptance of unearned privilege and power.

HERE IS WHAT I TELL my daughter about the ways I regard people of color and whites: Because of systems like the one at Texaco, the reasons why a person of color distrusts whites are fundamentally different from the reasons of a white person who distrusts people of color. The white person benefits from a system that supports his distrust in a way that the person of color does not. For example, the white person's distrust of people of color helps maintain predominantly white middle class suburbs where the schools receive financial support superior to those schools attended by the more racially mixed populations of the inner cities. This white distrust also helps keep environmental dangers from their children which the children in inner cities are more often exposed to.

The distrust whites feel towards people of color does nothing to change this situation. To make these two distrusts equivalent forms of prejudice is to engage in a racist act. This camouflages and ignores obvious differences in the way whites and people of color are treated in this society and the powers and privileges they receive. And yet even as I make these arguments my doubts remain. Why do I feel that the attempt to help my daughter to understand all this cannot be changed simply by arguments or reason, statistics or facts?

AT THE AGE OF FIVE, in every picture of me, I've got a pair of six guns cinched about my waist. Or else I'm pointing them at the camera, my black cowboy hat pushed back, my mouth snarling with a bravado and toughness I evinced only as a pose or when alone, walking down the dark steps of our apartment building out to the street. At each step I'd wave to the fans at the rodeo, shouting "Howdy folks," the way I imagined Roy Rodgers did stepping into the arena and onto Trigger, the

Wonder Horse. Before I went on to collect baseball cards, I collected cowboy cards, with the heroes from various television series, wrapped up together with a slice of chewing gum for a nickel: *Have Gun Will Travel*, *Sugarfoot, Maverick, Gene Autry, the Lone Ranger, The Rebel*, classic American icons of the fifties.

In one of my poems, I picture myself riding in the back of our Bel-Air, shooting at the glass, bouncing up and down in gunfight delirium, wearing the black cowboy hat and cold cocked steely gaze of Paladin, who'd leave his calling card, "Have Gun, Will Travel", everywhere he went. When my friend, the Japanese Canadian playwright, Rick Shiomi read the poem, he remarked, "Do you remember what happened at the beginning of that show? This Chinese guy with a pig tail would come running into the hotel lobby, shouting, 'Teragram for Mista Paradin, teragram for Mista Paradin'?"

I don't remember this Chinese messenger at all. All I see is Richard Boone striding down the stairs, the epitome of cowboy cool, his pencil thin mustache and tight glinting gaze.

How did I know I didn't want to be like this Chinese messenger? What did my disassociation from him, my erasure of his presence from my memory, say about the way I felt about myself, my own body, my identity as an Japanese American? I grew up as someone who wanted to assimilate into the white majority, who thought it a compliment when a white person would say to me in high school, "I think of you David just like a white person." From early on I perceived that the world felt there was something wrong about the way I looked, who I was as a Japanese, an Asian, a alien who could never quite be considered American, no matter how much I tried to pretend otherwise.

So how did all this affect the way I looked at whites and blacks? I remember this experience when I went to see the film *Out of Africa* in the Ginza during a year long visit in Japan during my early thirties. For months I'd been living in this environment where everybody looked like me, where I was in the visual majority, even if I wasn't Japanese. All this began to change the way I felt about myself, about my body and the way I looked. Very quickly

I started asking all sorts of questions about what race had meant to my identity in America.

And then I was watching this movie where Meryl Streep plays the Danish author Isak Dinesen. Early in the movie she travels to her Kenyan plantation for the first time. When she approaches the plantation, it is late at night and a crowd of Kenyan servants come up and greet her. As I watched this scene, suddenly I realized I was bored with Meryl Streep's face. I was bored with the white face at the center of the film. I had seen the white bwana in Africa over and over in films since I was a child. I knew that story. What I was really interested in was what was happening in the minds of the Kenyans. Their interior life. And I realized that all my cultural training had been to place the white face automatically at the center and to place the black faces in the margins. Suddenly I felt I wasn't doing this anymore. I was withdrawing affection, attention, and curiosity from that white face, and giving it to the black faces.

In that moment I realized that was a part of the way racism works. It's not only a question of whether you blatantly discriminate against people or not. It involves what happens when you see a face. How do you react emotionally? How does your psychic energy react? Does it go out to that face? What sort of assumptions does your psyche make about how interesting that person is going to be? How curious you are? How much affection do you feel? So much of that just happens in an instant, subconsciously. What conditions that reaction? How are children taught to identify themselves? To identify others? How do these identifications prevent us from seeing each other clearly? How to we learn new ways of understanding each other across racial lines?

Another story I've told Samantha:

ONE NIGHT I was talking in a bar with four black male friends, three writers and a theater director. These were men who had won prizes for their work, one had written for the "Cosby" show, another had written a bestselling novel; they were all college educated. At a certain point they began trading stories about how they had been picked up by the police for driving in a white neighborhood. I was struck by the fact that while the stories were laced at times with anger and a sense of humiliation, the dominant emotion was laughter. It was as if they were trading long familiar stories, filled with an absurd humor, stories which framed almost as initiations, something you could not escape if you were an African American male in America.

I grew up as a middle class Asian American. I lived in the white suburbs, places where my black artist friends could neither live nor drive. My experience had been totally different from my black male friends. If I felt a sense of alienation, a sense of being out of place, an odd anomaly and sexual misfit in my suburban high school, I never felt endangered by the police. I never heard from my father that it was hard for him to find a place in the suburbs where people like us could live (although such places did exist).

I have also talked to Samantha about standing outside a New York hotel with my best friend, Alexs, who's African American. After a few minutes, I decided no taxi was going to come down the street and I suggested to

Alexs that we walk up to Broadway and catch one. He turned to me and said, "Okay, we can do that. But I stand here because I know I might get a taxi here. If I go up to Broadway the taxis won't stop for me."

I've explained to Sam that when Alexs stands in front of the hotel the drivers think he's staying there and is not someone who might rob them. If he stands like everyone else on Broadway, all the taxi drivers see is a black man with dreadlocks, which sets them worrying that he might be a criminal.

I also relate what Alexs later said about this incident: "Now I know how to dress, how to look safe. But sometimes you just say to yourself, fuck it. I'll look just like that brother over there who is going to take you down. And it's your job to figure out if I'm an outlaw. And that's why I stay home a lot. That's why I stay in my house a lot. That's why when the phone, when the doorbell rings, I don't feel that good. I'm not anxious to see who is at my front door. I am never anxious to see who's at my front door. I won't go to the front door."

Finally, I told Sam that if Alexs stands on Broadway

in New York with me and tries to hail a cab that might be okay. I never seem to have trouble hailing cabs. And that's one difference between being an Asian American male and an African American male in this country. It's a difference I never understood much about growing up.

AT THE TIME Alexs and I first became friends I was engaged in a growing rift between me and several white friends, a group of fellow writers in the Twin Cities. The rift had started with an argument over *Miss Saigon* and my objections to the play, and to the fact that a white British actor, Jonathan Price, was given the role of a Eurasian without any Asian Americans even being allowed to try out for the part. This argument quickly spilled over into other racial issues. At the time I was identifying myself more and more as a Japanese American, an Asian American and a person of color, and I was shedding the desires for assimilation and whiteness that I had grown up with. As this happened and as I began speaking more and more about race in my public appearances as a writer, I noticed a curious phenomena: The things I had been saying which had caused difficulties with my white writer friends were the exact same things which seemed to cause people of color in my audiences to come up and talk to me after my appearances. It became clear to me that, in certain ways, I had to choose one group or the other.

I've written about this elsewhere, so I don't want to go into this here. What I do want to mention is that this was an incredibly painful process. I seemed to be having the same argument with almost every single white writer friend I had (they in turn had to have the argument only with me—I was the only writer of color in the group).

One day as I was talking to Alexs and he was advising me, I realized that he knew more about dealing with racism than I did. I also felt he understood me at that moment better than anyone I knew, including my wife, whom I knew loved me more than anyone else in the world and who is white.

At that moment I realized Alexs was psychologically more astute than I thought he was. Then I realized he was smarter than I thought he was. Then I realized I had not seen this before because of my own racism. I thought: If

I'm a person of color and I'm doing this to someone who's black, my whole view of racism needs to change.

I had until this point thought of Alexs as a bit bristly, a bit too quick too anger, someone with a chip on his shoulder. But, as we became friends, as he felt he could trust me more and more to try to understand his experiences rather than deny them or his interpretation of them, my vision, my interpretation of his world, changed. I realized that at the times I thought he was being too quick to anger, he was actually being restrained. After all, judging whether someone is too angry or not depends on whether you see all the reasons they have to be angry. I realized I did not see many of the reasons for Alexs' anger, his history of dealing with racism. Indeed, my whole education and cultural training had led me *not* to see these things. I came to view those moments when Alexs did raise his voice a bit, did allow his emotions to show, as great acts not just of restraint, but of survival, of tremendous will power, of spirituality and forbearance. Obviously my judgment of his character changed.

This, I tell my daughter, is one of the reasons why I

don't think it possible for most white people to judge the character of people of color. If they don't understand or see the world people of color live in, what experience they bring to the table, how can whites judge our actions at the table? How can they know why the person of color is reacting the way they do? How can they know the struggles we have gone through to get to the table?

In an article in *Vanity Fair* (May, 1998), Fran Leibowitz likened the competition between blacks and whites to a race. The white person sees the black person line up at the starting line and says, okay, let's have a fair race. If I win I'm the better qualified. But what the white person doesn't realize, argues Leibowitz, is that the black person has run several miles already to get to the starting line. It's not a fair race at all.

WHAT I HAVE BEEN SAYING HERE can be summed up in two basic sets of contradictions. They both involve what whites learn about race in our society.

Here is the first set of contradictory beliefs which exist within the psyche of most whites in this country:

1.   I believe white culture, white mores, are superior,
     and, in the end, I care more about what happens to
     white people than to black people. I have been
     taught through the culture and through my educa-
     tion that white people are superior to black people
     and are basically more important to me.

2.   I must judge people fairly and equally and not
     practice discrimination.

Now what happens when a white person with these
contradictory beliefs interacts with a black person? This is
what I believe occurs, and my belief is based on the fact that
this is also the way I was taught to think of black people:

The white person constantly tries to keep the second
tenet in mind—I judge people fairly, I'm not prejudiced.
But so much of that white person's cultural education
has taught him the opposite; therefore that training must
be kept from the focus of his consciousness.

Of course this attempt is problematic. At some conscious or sub-conscious level, the white person is aware
that he is trying to repress this first message. This makes

the white person very self-conscious. He is afraid of his own psyche; he fears that the part which thinks whites are superior, will somehow slip out, and he knows this must not happen.

The more contact the white and black person have, the more frank they become with each other, the more likely this first message will slip out. That is one reason why whites avoid intimacy with blacks.

And what happens when this first message slips out, when the white person reveals the message of white superiority that he has learned through the culture? When he shows the part of his psyche that thinks whites are more knowing and more important? The black person gets angry. And in turn the white person gets defensive or denies what he has said. Or retreats or feigns ignorance about what has angered the black person. In most cases the white person leaves the room psychically and often physically and does not come back to the relationship. The black person's anger brings up too much tension, points too directly to the contradictions within the white person's psyche.

Now the white person may not even be aware that he has let slip these beliefs about the superiority and importance of whites. After all, this is the part of his psyche that the white person wants to hide in any encounter with a black person.

In contrast the black person cannot hide from the existence of such a belief in the psyche of whites. A whole history of encounters the black person has had with whites and white institutions only point to the existence of such a belief. Richard Wright referred to this when he said that blacks have a song which says I can't believe what you say, because I see what you do.

What if whites were not frightened off by this anger and, more importantly, by the revelations of their own psyche? Perhaps they might be are able to cross color lines and achieve a truthfulness and intimacy that most relationships between blacks and whites in this country lack.

HERE IS THE SECOND PAIR of contradictory beliefs which the white person must deal with:

1. I benefit from a system which gives me special privileges as a white person and denies them to black people. All whites participate on some level in this system.

2. This country is a democracy, people are supposed to be judged as individuals and, in general, there is equality; only a few whites are really racists.

Here again, if the white person does not want to think herself a racist, she will cling to the second statement as a general truth and try to block out, to push from his consciousness the first statement. Yet, somewhere deep down in their psyches, whites know this first statement is true.

The sociologist Andrew Hacker routinely asks his white students this question: Say you accidently turned into a black during an operation—your features changed to an African American—and you will live approximately another 50 years. How much will you seek in compensation? Most of his white students seemed to feel "it would not be out of place to ask for $50 million, or $1 million a year. And this calculation conveys, as well as anything, the value that white people place on their own skins. Indeed, to be white is to possess a gift whose value can be appreciated only after it is taken away." (*Two Nations*, Andrew Hacker, Charles Scribner's Sons, 1992)

Again, when she is dealing with blacks, the white person will constantly propound the second statement, and deny the existence of the first statement or argue that it is false. But to the black person, the first statement is an obvious truth. It's much easier to see when someone is privileged if you don't share in those privileges. If you enjoy those privileges, they just seem a natural way of life, something you were born with.

In his book, *Savage Inequalities* (Harper Collins, 1991), Jonathan Kozol writes: "Total yearly spending—local funds combined with state assistance and the small amount that comes from Washington—ranges today [in Illinois from $2,100 on a child in the poorest district to above $10,000 in the richest. The system, writes John Coons, a professor of law at Berkeley University, 'bears the appearance of calculated unfairness.'

There is a belief advanced today, and in some cases by conservative black authors, that poor children and particularly black children should not be allowed to hear too much about these matters. If they learn how much less they are getting than rich children, we are told, this knowledge may induce them to regard themselves as 'victim,' and such 'victim-thinking,' it is argued, may then undermine their capability to profit from whatever opportunities may actually exist. But this is a matter of psychology—or strategy—and not reality. The matter, in any case, is academic since most adolescents in the poorest neighborhoods learn very soon that they are getting less than children in the wealthier school districts. They see suburban schools on television and they seem them when they travel for athletic competitions. It is a waste of time to worry whether we should tell them something they could tell us. About injustice, most poor children in America cannot be fooled."

Thus the two biggest psychological barriers to dealing with racism involve the denial of whites of their knowledge that the following statements contain an essential truth about their psyche and lives:

1. I believe white culture and whites are superior to and more important than blacks.

2. I benefit from a system which gives me special privileges as a white person and denies them to black people.

If you are white and can begin to investigate, even a little bit, how these two statements apply to you, and you continue in that investigation, you will know what you need to do to combat racism. You will figure out the next steps you need to take.

We have come to the point where people in our society recognize racist insults and blatant acts of discrimination as wrong. What then are the other ways through which racism works in our society?

Can there be unconscious acts of racism?

How does racism work on a group rather than individual level?

In what ways does racism work as a system of power and privilege?

What are the acts or beliefs that many people of color believe are racist and whites do not?

Why is there disagreement about which acts or beliefs may be labeled racist?

In what ways are a person's experience in our society determined by skin color?

How do these differences in experience affect the way a person looks at and interprets the world around them?

How do whites tend to view these differences in experience and interpretation?

How do African Americans? How do Asian Americans?

Can we make such generalizations? Do we need to?

HOW DO ASIAN AMERICANS fit into this picture of white-black relations? Obviously, that's a complicated question. Here's one way I've tried to explain this to my daughter:

In 1944, when my father was interned with other Japanese Americans at the internment camp in Jerome, Arkansas, he would sometimes be allowed a day pass to go to Little Rock to see a movie. At that time when he left the camp and stepped onto a local bus, the bus was segregated.

When I asked my father where he sat then, he said, "We sat in the front of the bus, where the whites sat." And at the lunch counter? "We sat where the whites sat." And at the movies? "We sat beneath the balcony, where the whites sat."

In certain ways this decision is quite understandable: You sit where the power is. You sit where your life is going to be more comfortable.

The Nisei (second generation Japanese American) journalist Bill Hosokowa wrote about this situation:

*The evacuees who were sent to Arkansas had been
astonished to find they were regarded as white by
the whites and colored by the blacks. The whites
insisted the Japanese Americans sit in front of the
bus, drink from the white man's fountain and use
the white man's rest rooms even though suspecting
their loyalty to the nation. And the blacks
embarrassed many a Nisei when they urged:
"Us colored folks has got to stick together." If there
was no middle ground in the South's polarized
society of black and white, in the rest of the country
after the war, a Nisei could live as a yellow-
skinned American without upsetting too many
people, and he also discovered it was not
particularly difficult to be accepted into the
white man's world. (Nisei: The Quiet Americans)*

What we notice here is the embarrassment Hosokawa
attributes to the Nisei when they are offered solidarity
with the blacks. We also see that after the war the Nisei
are interested in fitting into the white world and the
black world seems to not exist for them.

The implications of a Japanese American on this segregated bus are quite telling. For one thing, when my father steps on that bus, his identity is created not simply by his relations with his own community or with the white community who have seen him as a threat to American security and a perpetual alien. His identity is also created by the matrix of black-white relations.

When he sits in the front half of the bus, the whites grant him status as an "honorary white," with certain of the privileges that come from being white. But they grant him this status on two conditions:

First, he must accept that he probably won't sit in the very front of the bus and he will absolutely never be able to drive the bus. He must also understand that his cultural heritage is something to be left behind; it means nothing here.

Secondly, he must pay no attention to the people at the back of the bus, he must claim no relationship to the people at the back of the bus, and he must absolutely never ever protest what is happening to the people at the back of the bus.

Now this bargain, this honorary white status, is often still offered to Asian Americans. When we accept this bargain, other people of color in the back of the bus see our acceptance for what it is: an acceptance of the racial status quo. And they are, appropriately, angry at us for supporting a racist system.

When Asians immigrate to America, as so many have done since the immigration laws changed in 1965, nothing in Asian culture prepares them for what it means to be an Asian American, to look they way they do and live in America. At the same time they soon realize that the further down they are on the economic ladder the more they are regarded as being like the "blacks" and they soon sense what that means. After all they are exposed to the same education and stereotyped media as whites. Of course, they are not told how Asians became the model minority at the exact time blacks began protesting for their civil rights. They often do not know that doors are opened for them through anti-discrimination laws created by the efforts of African Americans. Instead many Asian Americans discover that the further they move up the economic ladder the greater the opportunities to become "honorary whites."

I was no different than my father, I tell my daughter. For a long time I wanted to be an "honorary white." Then I saw I needed to fight that wish, the price of the ticket. And everything changed.

WHEN MY DAUGHTER READ Ben Jelloun's essay, she told me she found parts interesting, such as the discussion of cloning or the history of the word "ghetto," but most of it already felt familiar to her.

Some of this I suppose is because she's only nine years old. She says she doesn't hear racist insults toward any groups at school. The school she goes to is very racially mixed and also includes students from recent immigrant groups. No one group really predominates. She knows there are other schools and areas where there are more racial tensions but for now it doesn't play a big role in her life. A friend who has an older son has told me that at Samantha's school, it is in the junior high, when boy-girl parties start to happen, that racial segregation starts to set in. When I told Samantha this it didn't really register; boy-girl parties seem a long way off to her in fourth grade.

Just after I finished this essay, she and I had another discussion that started because of the issue of redistricting and busing in the Minneapolis suburbs. She'd read a letter to the editor where a white woman argued that the residents of her suburb were unfairly being branded as racists. In the course of our talk Samantha—ever vigilant against unwarranted generalizations—accused me of saying that all the people in the suburbs were racists. "I know for a fact that that's not so," she said. "You can't say that. Do you know everyone that lives there? That's just the same as the people from the suburbs saying everyone who lives in the city is a gang-banger. It's not like everyone in the suburbs is racist and everyone in the city is for diversity and isn't prejudiced."

We finally settled upon the statement that perhaps there were more people in the suburbs who were racists than those in the suburbs believed. (After all, if the suburbs were so free of racism, wouldn't people of color be flocking there in droves?) I told Samantha that this issue in part depend d upon the way you define racism and I went over some points I've tried to make here. I think the stories about myself, my friend Alexs or other friends, stories she's heard before about people she knows, affected her. But whenever I got into something abstract like the systematic nature of racism, she tuned out. At one point she said, "How old were you when the first man stepped on the moon?" As I'm wont to do I ignored this signal to change the subject and plowed on stubbornly until she said again, "It must have really interesting when the first man stepped on the moon." The discussion was over. She was bored. I'd gone on too long.

Part of me suspects that our conversation had as much to do with the fact that she'd recently come home from a trip to Japan with her mother and our discussion was simply a way of our re-connecting. And I realize that she sometimes says things which she knows I'll counter, just to see what my arguments are and to test her own sense of independence. In the end, she'll need to discover or create a way of looking at these matters that's hers and not mine, some new way not encapsulated either by my beliefs or the more conservative beliefs she's exposed to at school and through the media.

Still, I'm left with this question: When she's older, how much will she read our conversations as Dad ranting and how much as necessary discussions over a crucial issue? I just hope it's some mixture of both.

William Ayers with his sons, Chesa Jackson, Zayd Osceola, and Malik Cochise.

Jim Shames

To the Bone: Reflections in Black and White

A RESPONSE TO TAHAR BEN JELLOUN

WILLIAM AYERS

A CHILD'S QUESTION: I am riding an early morning bus in New York City with my son Zayd, five years old and just beginning to read. The bus is packed with commuters, the mood a resigned grumpiness. Only Zayd is bright-eyed and chirpy as we groan down the avenue toward school and work. "Poppy," Zayd says in his large outside voice, turning to me expectantly. "What's a kike?" A hush falls as two hundred eyes lift and, in the sudden silence, begin to sizzle, laser-like, into my head.

What?

"A kike. What's a kike?"

I freeze. I seize up. I buy time: "Where did you hear that word, Zayd?"

"I read it," he replies proudly. "See?" He points to a

stab of red graffiti slashed across a rear window. "*I HATE KIKES*," it reads—all upper case—and it is punctuated with a swastika.

"A kike..." I stammer. "A kike..." I search my erratic mind. I pursue my elusive courage. And then, miraculously, the crowd recedes, and there is only Zayd with his basic trust intact, his childish hope undiminished, alive, his deeply human sense-making engine firing on all cylinders, and I know I must respond simply but honestly, for his sake and for my own.

"Kike," I begin in a clear voice, "is a word full of hatred. It's a word full of violence, a word used by people who want to hurt Jews, like the word 'nigger' is meant to hurt black people. It's a lying word, because it says that some people are more human than others, that some groups are superior to others, that some are less than human. Some people, filled up with hate, might call you a 'kike'. It's the kind of word we should never use, the kind of word we must always object to and oppose."

Zayd's face never loses its open and intent concentration. "OK," he says simply. "Should you cross it out?"

What a thought! I drag a magic marker from my backpack, walk over and obliterate the stain. "OK," he says again as I turn to face a smiling crowd, a few thumbs ups, and an audible collective sigh.

A child's questions: Why is the floor sticky? Why is the sky blue? Why do balls bounce? Why is that man sleeping in the street? Why is that woman bleeding? Why is my skin brown? A child's questions innocently ask us to reconsider the world, to confront our own gaps and ignorance, to rethink the taken-for-granted, the habitual, our insistent common sense. Their questions can be disruptive and disquieting, to be sure, which may explain the knee-jerk answers we hear ourselves repeating: I'll tell you later, or when you're older, or when I have more time, or don't ask. Our avoidance reveals our incomprehension, perhaps, but, as well, the fierce embrace of our personal dogmas, our easy beliefs. And it brings us face to face with our own temerity—it is frightening, after all, to open every door, to doubt every truth, to wonder again at every mystery. "I'll tell you later"—the door slams shut and we sigh with relief as the illusion of safety descends.

Children's questions can, on the other hand, shock us into new awarenesses—if we allow them to. The ground shifts and we are forced (or invited) to make sense again of all that is before us, to dig deeper perhaps, to discover something truer, more layered, more nuanced, more complex. If we take their questions in this way, they may become occasions for the ethical to emerge. We begin to notice the obstacles blocking the paths of human beings toward freedom, toward fulfillment and wholeness in their humanness, and we wonder how to name those obstacles, how to choose ourselves in opposition, how to reach out and link up with others in acts of repair. We move then beyond the facticity of the here and now toward a future our children will shape and inhabit. Our social imaginations are engaged—can we envision a better social order? Can we conceive a decent world, a place fit for all our children? Can we dream a site of peace and justice?—and we begin to speak a normative language, an idiom of "should" and "ought." And then, if we are open enough and if the catalyst tugs hard enough, we can be stirred to action. I would have left the gruesome graffiti alone, after all, (as

did a hundred fellow travelers) had I not been prodded by
a fresh-faced five-year-old whom I loved intensely and
who, without any drama or theatrics, just assumed that his
Poppy would do the right thing.

Tahar Ben Jelloun is drawn to the ravine of race, to
the treacherous rift of racism, provoked into the breach
now by an attractive and powerful agent: his own ten-
year-old child. The spark is her searching curiosity as she
marches in a demonstration hand in hand with Ben Jelloun through the streets of Paris. What is racism? she
begins. What is race? Prejudice? Culture? A scapegoat?
Genocide? Heredity? Genes? An ethnic group? One
childish question leaps to another and another, and Ben
Jelloun, to our collective benefit, keeps pace with her
curiosity, pushes through the cotton wool of shackled
consciousness, the pseudo-language of clichés and
slogans, to offer simple responses we can weigh and
wonder about. Take it as a guide and a conversation.

What is racism?

Each of us could, of course, write a book about race.
Mine begins with my own childish question: "Why is

Celeste brown?" Celeste cleaned our house and I had noticed something—a difference. "Shush," my mother scolded. "We don't talk that way." Growing up in an entirely constructed racialized surround, and one in which almost no white person acknowledges its existence, means that we draw a common-sense experience of race into ourselves with our every breath, that we drink it in, beginning with our mother's milk. A society founded on the attempted genocide of the original people, built on the labor of African slaves, developed by Latino serfs and Asian indentured servants, made fabulously wealthy through conquest and exploitation, manipulation and mystification —a society like this one is a society built on race.

But race is unspeakable. "We don't talk that way." I'll say. We don't talk at all. I remember a moment of muteness when my three kids came home one day from junior high school with a story of a fist-fight in the cafeteria. "Paul called Tony a 'pollack,' and then Tony called Paul a 'nigger,'" Zayd reported, "and then they really got into it." After describing the fight and noting that both boys were suspended from school, they wanted to know, "Which is

worse, 'pollack' or 'nigger'?" What do you think? I coun-
tered, buying time once again. They had studied the Indian
wars, the slave trade, and the Holocaust in Europe, and so
we had a lengthy, engaged talk about the historical weight
of words, the ways in which meaning can link to power
and control, why calling a Jew a name in Germany, for
example, might resonate with additional power. "Why do
the black kids call each other 'nigger'?" one of them then
asked, and this led to an involved discussion of both the
co-optation and the sometimes internalization of hateful
language. When I went to their school to urge a broader
discussion so that all the kids could benefit from reflection
on these difficult and complex issues, issues already abuzz
in the informal curriculum of the cafeteria, I was told that
talk would be troublesome. "We don't have a race problem
here," the principal assured me, "And this might stir something up. Besides," she continued, playing to other fears
"math exams are coming up." A teachable moment dis-
carded, lost. And in that screaming silence a lens of distorted images, fears, misunderstandings, and cool calculat-
edness slips neatly into place. We are, each of us, born into

race and place, and all the early lessons are about knowing something of each. But we are rendered speechless.

Frederick Douglass, the great American abolitionist, found the roots of bigotry in the need to justify oppression:

> *Pride and selfishness... never want for a theory to justify them—and when men oppress their fellow-men, the oppressor ever finds, in the character of the oppressed, a full justification for his oppression. Ignorance and depravity, and the inability to rise from degradation to civilization and respectability, are the most usual allegations against the oppressed. The evils most fostered by slavery and oppression are precisely those which slaveholders and oppressors would transfer from their system to the inherent character of their victims. Thus the very crimes of slavery become slavery's best defense. By making the enslaved a character fit only for slavery, they excuse themselves for refusing to make the slave a free man. A wholesale method of accomplishing this result is to overthrow the instinctive consciousness of the common brotherhood of man....**

* As quoted in Gates, Jr., H. L., "Why Now?" in Fraser, S. (ed.) *The Bell Curve Wars* (New York: Basic Books, 1995), p. 94.

In other words, the edifice of racism as bigotry is built upon the hard ground of race as a convenient invention for exploitation.

Prejudice and the idea of inferiority based on race, then, grow from and are fed by the need to justify and perpetuate inequality, domination, control. And while discrimination and slavery go back to antiquity, chattel slavery based on race—that is, the enslavement of an entire people and their transformation into commodities without any family, property, or rights whatsoever, bound for life and for generations into the imaginable future, and simultaneously the invention of whiteness as an immutable marker of privilege—is the "peculiar institution" born in North America of the African slave trade. Racism as a primary social and cultural dividing line in the United States— developed from a greed for profit and achieved by deception and a monopoly of firearms, not by biological superiority, real or imagined—is the legacy of that institution.

That is some of what W. E. B. Du Bois had in mind when he declared the problem of the twentieth century "the problem of the color line." As we approach the end of this century—a century marked by unparalleled degradation and violence against people because of color, ethnic background, and national origin, and by extraordinary efforts on the part of the downtrodden and disadvantaged of the earth to achieve and extend human dignity and freedom—Du Bois's words remain as lucid and significant as ever. "The problem of the color line," is more acute and entangled than ever, and requires an even more decisive response if Du Bois's twentieth century problem is not to define and distort the twenty-first.

Racism is a many-horned devil, to be sure, a many-fisted monster, and a thoughtful response must necessarily be multidimensional. Racism is a disease, perhaps a pathology. It is a sort of group madness, a kind of collective nervous break-down. It is a myth, a lie (a white lie or a black lie), a distortion. It is an evil out there in the world with a strong life of its own. It is ignorance, blindness, witlessness. And it is more.

Racism can be found in our language. Look at the dictionary, a seemingly authoritative source. Under "white" we find "free from spot or blemish," "free from moral impurity," "not intended to cause harm," "innocent," "marked by upright fairness;" and then phrases like "white knight," "white horse," and "white hope." "Black" doesn't fare so well: "dirty," "soiled," "thoroughly sinister or evil," "wicked," "sad, gloomy, or calamitous," "grim, distorted, or grotesque." Associated terms include black art (sorcery), black and blue (discolored from bruising), blackball (to exclude from membership), blackmail (to extort by threats), black market (illicit trade), black out (to envelop in darkness), black heart (evil), black day (characterized by disaster), and so on.

There it is, embedded in our language, the core of our ability to think and act with some semblance of harmony with others. A coward is "yellow," a victim of fraud is "gypped" or "Jewed." In a country brutally divided along racial lines, founded and sustained on a constructed hierarchy of color and calamitous class divisions, language itself is encoded with privilege, oppression, bias, bigotry, and power. Modern American English tells us who we are, where we have been, and where we are going. Is it any wonder?

I taught for several years in a school where we worked diligently to create a liberating and empowering environment for young children, and we struggled constantly with our own language. The school was founded and directed by an extraordinary young woman renowned for her advocacy of multicultural and anti-bias perspectives; the multiracial community of parents and staff tended toward public activism for equity and social justice. We wanted, as well, to free ourselves from the artificial constraints of a racist and sexist society, and so it became natural and not jarring in our school to hear conversation laced with terms like "mail carrier," "police officer," "cowhand," and, my personal favorite, "waitron." Not only did "firefighter" replace "fireman" but our dramatic play area had a poster of a black firefighter in action, and our block area had a unique collection of little figures including a white male nurse and a black woman firefighter. "Firefighter, firefighter, firefighter."

Now, here's the problem: Our school was across the street from a firehouse and the firehouse was staffed exclusively with white, male firemen. We visited the firefighters, tried on their hats, rang the bell, and got to know a few of them. One day Caitlin, five-years-old, asked Jimmy, the fireman, when he expected there would be women in the station house, and he exploded in laughter: "Never, I hope. Women can't do this work. The neighborhood would burn down."

"That's not fair," Caitlin said later, and the class wrote letters of protest to the fire chief, the mayor, and the city council pleading for justice, for the simple right of women to fight fires. Children are, of course, careful observers, diligent classifiers, and concrete learners, and reality is their most powerful teacher. Our non-sexist language and our non-racist materials were in combat with some hard facts, and changing language did not in itself change worlds. Our adult responsibility as far as their education is concerned includes the obligation to present the concrete situations they encounter as problems which challenge them and call for a response. The children of Little Rock or Soweto or our little school show us the possibility of this type of education, and of children as actors in history, not merely observers or objects or victims.

Toni Morrison talks of the "evacuated language" of the powerful, of the "systematic looting of language" geared toward "menace and subjugation." "Oppressive language does more than represent violence," she writes, "it is violence; does more than represent the limits of knowledge; it limits knowledge." She argues for the rejection and exposure of "obscuring state language or the faux language of mindless media," "language designed for the estrangement of minorities, hiding its racist plunder in its literary cheek." She describes "sexist language, racist language, theistic language" as "typical of the policing languages of mastery" that "cannot, do not, permit new knowledge or encourage the mutual exchange of ideas."*

Another child's question. Malik, our verbal, expressive three-year old, attends the preschool where I teach. Part of the normal experience of youngsters in this community is active involvement in neighborhood events and activities. Soon we will attend a pow-wow at a nearby junior high school sponsored by the American Indian Movement.

* Toni Morrison, Acceptance Speech to the Swedish Academy on the Occasion of the Awarding of the Nobel Prize in Literature, 1993. Reprinted by permission of International Creative Management, Inc. © 1993 Alfred A. Knopf, Inc.

When I tell the kids about the pow-wow they are
excited and eager. There will be drums; there will be
food to eat. But Malik, who typically loves ritual, wants
none of it. He whispers to me: "Will the Indians be wild,
Poppy? Will they be scary?" No, I assure him. It will be
engaging and interesting and we will have a good time.
And we do. But Malik insists that I hold him for the first
hour, just to be sure.

Where did he get the idea that the Indians would be
wild or scary? He's only three, after all, and we don't even
own a television. He is named for Malcolm X (in Arabic,
Malik el Shabazz) and his middle name is Cochise; he
has pictures of Malcolm X and Cochise in his room, and
has read from our extensive collection of positive children's books about Native Americans. How did this
stereotype get into his head?

Of course, we have all seen the children's books filled
with headdresses and hatchets; I remember an alphabet
book with "I" for "Imitating Indians," and the accompany-
ing illustration of animals whooping around and acting
crazy—I think of a whole book modeled on this one entry:

"J" for "Jumping Jews" wearing yarmulkes, or "N" for "Nice Negroes" eating watermelon. Disgusting. All Americans are part of the culture of disappearing Indians (ten little, nine little, eight little Indians—a particularly appalling children's song filled with suggestions of genocide), wooden Indians, Indian-givers, drunken Indians, cowboys and Indians, and all the rest. Most of us encounter *Little House on the Prairie* at some point, with Laura Ingalls Wilders' shivery description of the wild, stinking, animal-like Indians of her imagination. We learn that Indians are somehow the enemy. We are set up, then, to accept the crass justifications for piracy and murder. Where do we get these ideas? They are, of course, knit deeply into the fabric of our culture: they are a toxic substance in the air we breathe; they come without asking and are available without effort. They are put in our heads early and often.

And so there is language, racist language and the language of racists, and still there is more. Language is not yet the bottom of the matter; it reflects, it mirrors, but it is neither fountainhead nor generator. We must, then, at some point push beyond language, go through the looking glass, as it were, in search of the source of such vivid and enduring speech.

Race bristles with significance, and yet when we speak of race we pull from a curious variety of meanings and a cacophonous base of knowledge. Race might refer, and often does, to a people or nation or tribe of the same stock and background—the German race, the Jewish race, the Japanese race, the French race, the American race. That this has a preposterous edge comes as no surprise, for practically no one really believes any longer that those broad strokes of background are somehow immutable or implacable, that tribal stock is really static, or that national identity is stone-like. And yet, not so long ago crime statistics in Chicago, for example, were broken down into categories that strike us today as odd: Irish, Italian, Jewish, Negro, white. They are now reported as Black, White, Hispanic, Asian. It all depends on the lens, on the angle of regard. It is hard, however, to claim much in the way of progress here.

In truth, human beings permeate each other fairly freely, collide and burrow, pierce and enter one another in an enduring and dynamic dance of change and inter-change. And it has always been so: we meet, we mate. Because we can, we do, and we are, then, of a single race: human. There are no other races, pure and simple.

Poets remind us of this ancient truth. Here is Langston Hughes:

> *Consider me,*
> *A colored boy,*
> *Once sixteen,*
> *Once five, once three,*
> *Once nobody,*
> *Now me.*
> *Before me*
> *Papa, mama,*
> *Grandpa, grandma,*
> *So on back*
> *To original*
> *Pa...*
> *Consider me,*
> *Descended also*
> *From the*
> *Mystery.*[*]

ALL THE ATTEMPTS through the centuries to divide
human beings into the fiction of races—173 in one scientific rendering two hundred years ago, 57 in another
—would seem silly if they didn't represent such murderous and bloody projects. But they always do. The invention
of whiteness as a permanent symbol of the fully-human,
the just-us, as a chit to be traded on in tough times, is the
condition that creates the other, the stranger, the less-
than-fully-human. David Malouf, in *Remembering Babylon*,
describes the unraveling of a settler community on the
Queensland coast of Australia when a man stumbles from
the out-back who looks and talks like a native, but is,
unmistakably, an Englishman who had been raised by
Aboriginals from boyhood—without the neat division of
"us" and "other" the town spins out of control. Wherever
we find the marshalling of science to define visible human
differences as races, we find conquest on the agenda and
ruin at the horizon. The invention and glorification of race
is ultimately a recipe for murder.

Every story of oppression begins with the cries and
groans of unjustified suffering, undeserved harm,

unnecessary pain—stories of human beings in chains or under the boot. It begins, say, with slavery, not an American invention, but, rather, a frightening commonplace in human experience. Americans, even today, like to point glibly to slavery's historic banality, its everydayness through the ages, as if that trumps the "peculiar institution" slavery became in our own land, in the hands of our forefathers.

A word, especially one that points to something so large and so ghastly, can conceal as much as it reveals, can in spite of itself, provide a protective gloss so that the unspeakable—in being spoken—is reduced and falsified. War, genocide, slavery—we search out the words to name the world, to understand, to see, to grasp, perhaps to change all that we find before us. But sometimes, through misuse or overuse, words become clichés, then slogans. The rough edges, the specificity is sanded off and smoothed out; we utter the word without weeping. The imagination collapses and the mind closes down. Whatever horror the word pointed to in the first place becomes opaque; the word blinds us, erases the world.

Just so, slavery. It is large, it is long. It is dreadful; we can all agree there. But it has come to a condition of little depth, little detail.

So think of this particular young man, a young man with a specific human face, a mother and a father, a past and a future. He has a name that points to his ancestors, his father's father's name, and beckons toward a future of promise and redemption. He is in love, for the first time perhaps, and his new wife is pregnant with their first child, a sign of productivity and abundance, their hope for tomorrow. He works every day in the fields and the forests, minding crops and animals, gathering food, attending to the requirements of his home and his village. Almost every evening he smokes his pipe with the men before he rests.

And then in one blinding and violent moment his life is crushed. The sudden, searing struggle overwhelms him, cripples him, leaves him bloody and gasping. Whipped and chained and transported in the hold of a ship for thirty-four torturous days of puking and dying and starving and shitting, he arrives in a strange and brutal place only half alive.

He endures, he survives. The pain is never entirely gone, but the mind shuts down and covers up, the raw and open wounds become scars. He lives for forty-two more years, fathers two more children but knows neither one, dies without family or mourners, his remains placed in an unmarked slave yard near the fields.

How can we understand such a thing? Everything the young man had was taken, but more than this. Everything he was, everything he might have become was also stolen from him. What footprint did he leave in the sand? What meaning did he make? In slavery the attempt was made to transform him from a person of depth and dimension to a thing for the use of others. His humanity was reduced by the slave traders to a crude cash transaction, his hopes and dreams, his aspirations and capacities smashed on the ground.

This single act is a monstrous crime, of course. But, rather than multiply this single crime by, say, ten million lives, better to take it life by human life, each story specific in its horror, each particular. The telling of it makes the pain distinct, understandable in human terms.

And then there is the slave trader's side of the story, the birth of institutional racism. I remember a film tracing a family's history back to Africa. Early in the story, the captain of a slave ship, a man who considers himself a Christian and a liberal and finds, he claims, the transporting of slaves odious work, confronts his first mate, a crude, unpolished fellow who regularly rapes and abuses the human cargo, often throwing people who resist overboard, and taunting the captain for his squeamishness. The captain, all worry and hand-wringing, implores the brute to treat the slaves a bit better, insisting that they are also human beings and God's children. The first mate looks him squarely in the eye and responds with astounding lucidity: of course they're human beings, he says, and if we're to profit from this enterprise we'd best convince them and everyone else that they're dogs or mules, anything but human. You see, he points out, if they're fully human, there's absolutely no justification for our business. Only if they're inferior—in their own minds *and* in the minds of the exploited but relatively advantaged whites—will we stand to gain. We must, if we are to benefit, insist that they are "niggers." With that the captain retreats into his ineffectual anguish.

It begins with human beings mistreating others and then codifying and justifying that mistreatment in law and institutions. James Baldwin wrote that, "the brutality with which Negroes are treated in this country cannot be overstated, however unwilling white men may be to hear it." It begins in the real world, the blood and bone world, in the world of concrete material things.

In other words, while racism is indeed a bad idea, it is an idea brought forth and sustained by a rotten reality. The bad idea is not its own source nor foundation. Rather it pivots on a base of injustice and operates simultaneously on many levels—the imposition of white supremacy is then rationalized by religion, culture, and myth, encoded in law, defended by force and violence. Fighting racism in the realm of language alone, or only in the world of ideas, without undermining the unjust structures that give birth to those ideas, is in the end a hopeless mission.

The endurance and strength of prejudiced ideas and values lies in their renewable life-source: the edifice of inequality based on color, the structures of privilege and oppression linked to race and backed up by force. In Illinois, for example, we have created what amounts to two parallel school systems—one privileged, stable, well-financed, and largely white, the other ineffective, chaotic, disadvantaged in countless ways, and largely African American, Latino, and poor. Racism is expressed through this duality, through inadequate resources for those most in need, through isolation, through unresponsiveness. When Governor James Thompson called Chicago schools "a black hole" while refusing to release more funds, he excited all the racist justifications that flow from and are fed by that unjust reality. Politicians continue to call Chicago schools "a rat hole," "a sink hole," and "a black hole"—rotten and bigoted language propping up a rotten and unequal structure.

Changing ideas and changing reality are quite distinct. The life blood of bigotry is the concrete situation it supports, but, it is also true that when an idea is the accepted currency of a large enough number of people, it becomes a force of its own, with a real, palpable power over people's lives. For example, when virtually all of Europe believed the world was flat, that belief became itself a barrier beyond which exploration proved impossible. To break through the barrier required an assault on the old idea, but it was the actual going beyond the edge of the earth that proved decisive in discrediting and eventually destroying the incorrect idea.

The world of children is not neatly bounded from other worlds and larger realities, and the explorations of children are neither logical nor discrete. They explore the world, and their inquisitive wanderings are organic and unlimited. They know no bounds. One of the challenging and refreshing things about living with children is that they go on exploring, asking about whatever enters their fields without regard to what is controversial or what is in bad taste or what is off limits. Children's comments are often dazzling in their insightfulness and their questions are often confounding in their illumination of human mystery. Why is mom angry? Why didn't dad come home last night? Why is he talking so loudly? Why is she in a wheelchair? Why is she asking for money? Is that fair?

Because racism is rooted in real (not imagined) oppression, and because that oppression is reflected in actual (not fantasy) inequality and injustice, it is not surprising that children discover the hard lessons about race and social value early. Kenneth and Mamie Clark showed with poignant clarity that black preschool children understood not only that they were black, but that to be white was an advantage in our society. By the age of four, children of all backgrounds tend to know who has cultural power and who has not, who to befriend and who to fear, who to choose and who to refuse.

This confronts teachers and educators with an enormous teaching problem. Because education at its best creates public spaces for people to come together with their own hopes and dreams and aspirations and experiences, education is essentially a process that opens doors and opens minds—anything that constrains or limits or closes is the enemy of education. Racism, sexism, homophobia, and other forms of organized oppression are anti-education. For this reason alone teachers and educators must struggle for ways to understand, engage with and resist racism in their classrooms and in the larger world.

What is to be done?

I am drawn to another explanation offered a child from another prominent novelist and searing essayist. This one was in the form of a "Letter to My Nephew on the One Hundredth Anniversary of the Emancipation," and I, although eavesdropping, read and re-read it, captivated, in my youth. The author was the incomparable James Baldwin, and the letter, "My Dungeon Shook" is the opening pages of *The Fire Next Time*. Baldwin wastes no time indicting the United States: "This is the crime of which I accuse my country and my countrymen, and for which neither I nor time nor history will ever forgive them," he begins, "that they have destroyed and are destroying hundreds of thousands of lives and do not know it and do not want to know it." Baldwin amasses a bill of particulars: "You were born where you were born and faced the future that you faced because you were black and for no other reason... You were born into a society which spelled out with brutal clarity, and in as many ways as possible, that you were a worthless human being." He tells his nephew that "it was intended that you should perish in the ghetto, perish by never being allowed to go beyond the white man's definitions, by never being allowed to spell your proper name." Baldwin argues that even though, "the details and symbols of your life have been deliberately constructed to make you believe what white people say about you," that his nephew—along with other black people—must "remember that what they believe, as well as what they do and cause you to endure, does not testify to your inferiority but to their inhumanity and fear." Too many white people, Baldwin believes, "are, in effect, still trapped in a history which they do not understand, and until they understand it, they cannot be released from it."

For Baldwin the remedy is painful and complex but available—Americans must look unblinkingly at our history, face our constructed reality, confront the tears of the wounded, the consequences of wickedness; we must harness ourselves, then, to a great collective effort toward justice. Baldwin finds hope in an image of, "the relatively conscious whites and the relatively conscious blacks, who must, like lovers, insist on, or create, the consciousness of the others in order to end the racial nightmare, and achieve our country." Action and commitment fueled by both rage and love, yes, but nothing until we summon the courage to look honestly at the world as it is: "it is not permissible that the authors of devastation should also be innocent. It is the innocence which constitutes the crime;" and "we, with love, shall force our brothers to see themselves as they are, to cease fleeing from reality and begin to change it."*

We must, then, at some point come face to face with the world as it really is. We see, then, that race is simultaneously a vast fiction and our most enduring and profound truth. We fight to see through and beyond the fabrication of race, even as we must note without equivocation the powerful consequences of our humanly constituted, profoundly racialized world—*both*. We cannot pretend to be colorblind, but neither can we stumble in our attempts to transcend race.

---

* Baldwin, James (1995) from *The Fire Next Time*, (New York: The Modern Library) pp 3–10. Reprinted with permission

The Nobel Laureate Wislawa Szymborska slices us
humans up into various weird categories and then hits us
with this deep, direct truth of our condition:

Out of every hundred people,
Those who always know better:
Fifty-two.
Unsure of every step:
Almost all the rest.
Ready to help,
If it doesn't take long:
Forty-nine.
Always good,
Because they cannot be otherwise:
Four — well, maybe five...
Able to admire without envy:
Eighteen.
Led to error
By youth (which passes):
Sixty, plus or minus.
Those not to be messed with:
Four and forty...
Harmless alone,
Turning savage in crowds:
More than half, for sure.
Cruel

When forced by circumstances:
It's better not to know,
Not even approximately...
Those who are just:
Quite a few, thirty-five
But if it takes effort to understand:
Three.
Worthy of empathy
Ninety-nine.
Mortal:
One hundred out of one hundred—
*A figure that has never varied yet.**

FACING REALITY fully involves confronting our history, embracing our past, including its deceptions and its discontents, its dishonesties and its disasters. We see, then, that racism is not a little secondary sub-plot in the American story but a central and permanent theme coloring every other. We wake up, we open our eyes. We are not innocent, then, but neither are we paralyzed. As the legal scholar Derrick Bell writes, "Perhaps those of us who can admit we are imprisoned by the history of racial subordination in America can accept — as slaves had no choice

---

* Szymborska, W. (1997) "A Word on Statistics," *Atlantic Monthly,* Vol. 279, no. 5, pg. 68.

but to accept — our fate. Not that we legitimate the racism of the oppressor. On the contrary, we can only delegitimate it if we can accurately pinpoint it. And racism lies at the center, not the periphery; in the permanent, not in the fleeting; in the real lives of black and white people, not in the sentimental caverns of the mind." Racism is a main channel in the North American river, not a small trickle at the edge.

For Bell, this recognition is not cause for despair, but rather for "engagement and commitment," and calls forth the same demand that black people have faced since slavery: "making something out of nothing. Carving out a humanity for oneself with absolutely nothing to help— save imagination, will, and unbelievable strength and courage. Beating the odds while firmly believing in, knowing as only they could know, the fact that all those odds are stacked against them." Bell urges action to create meaning, to name oneself in opposition, to oppose the void. He counsels "the pragmatic recognition that

* Bell, D. (1992) *Faces at the Bottom of the Well*, N.Y.: Basic Books, pp. 197-8.
Reprinted with permission.

racism is permanent" side by side with "the unalterable conviction that something must be done, that action must be taken."*

We must stand up to oppose the evil of racism, an evil that is out there in the world as surely as it is in here, inside our minds and our hearts. But because it is out there, it is foolish to parse matters—I'm better than Mark Fuhrman, we're tempted to boast, I'm neither a Nazi nor a Klansman. The important thing is not to slide off into self-congratulation, but is rather to find the courage to be counted, to stir from indifference and inaction, to love the world enough to oppose the evil. Baldwin, again: "It is not necessary that people be wicked, but only that they be spineless" to bring us all to wrack and ruin. Amilcar Cabral, the African liberationist, noted, on the other hand, that you don't need to be a hero today to change the world; it is enough to be honest.

Those who embrace this colossal effort will be assist-ed if we will employ a two-eyed approach: one eye fixed firmly on the world as it is, the other looking toward a world that could be but is not yet—a future fit for all our children, a place of peace and justice. We can, with bell hooks, learn to create little sites of freedom, small locations of possibility: "to labor for freedom, to demand of ourselves and our comrades, an openness of mind and heart that allows us to face reality even as we collectively imagine ways to move beyond boundaries, to transgress. This is education as the practice of freedom."* We can, with Tahar Ben Jelloun, respond to our children's questions directly and honestly. We can identify obstacles to our collective well-being and link up with others in simple acts of hope and love. We can, then, reclaim our humanity and, perhaps, as Baldwin would have it, achieve our country. This is surely worth our toil; it is worth our trouble.

* hooks, b. (1994) *Teaching to Transgress*, N.Y.: Routledge, p. 207. Reprinted with permission.

Lisa D. Delpit with her daughter, Maya

A Letter to My Daughter
on the Occasion of Considering
Racism in the United States

LISA DELPIT

When I read Tahar Ben Jelloun's Racism Explained to My
Daughter, *I considered my own nine year-old and what I
would want to say to her. Ben Jelloun says he wanted his text to
be "simple and objective." I've thought about that. I don't know
if there is anything I can say to my child that is either simple or
objective. Issues surrounding color and race in America are
very complex, and all of it hurts too much to even think about
objectivity. Even though she will not be able to understand this
letter yet without some help, I want her eventually to understand the pain of racism, the necessity for constant surveillance
lest it slip into our souls, and the torment that I, her mother,
face each time I am confronted with its ugly face.*

My Dearest Maya,

You are so amazing. Your golden brown skin, your deep black "ackee" eyes, your wiry, gold-flecked hair that seems persistently unwilling to stay contained in any manner of braid or twist I devise. I watch you move—the strength of your long limbs, the fluidity of your hips, your arms. I listen in amazement at your interpretations of the world, and laugh (but not quite as loudly as you) at your corny nine year-old jokes. I can't fathom how you've managed to turn those little baby digits I loved to kiss into the long, graceful fingers— adorned at the tips in blue and purple designer colors—that now dance so expertly across your violin strings. Yes, you are amazing.

As much as I think of you as my gift to the world, I am constantly made aware that there are those who see you otherwise. This country we live in is steeped in perverse contradictions about race and color. Its tragic history of slavery, its horrendous record of lynchings and other violence inflicted upon its darker citizens, its sad tradition of segregation all have all left a legacy of psyches torn apart with contradictions. Fear, anger, guilt, and a sense of white-skinned entitlement commingle to drive wedges between public words and private actions. Thomas Jefferson wrote the words, "All men are created equal" while he owned slaves. The city manager of our small community has publicly declared that he wants to live in an integrated community, yet is presently being investigated for supposedly having stated that what would make the police officer's patch even better than its present design (the Georgia State flag furled so as to accentuate its main focal point—the symbol of the Confederacy) would be a new design highlighting "a nigger hanging from a noose."

Although you don't realize it yet, it is solely because of your color that the police officers in our predominantly white neighborhood stop you to "talk" when you walk our dog. You think they're being friendly, but when you tell me that one of their first questions is always, "Do you live around here?" I know that they question your right to be here, that somehow your being here threatens their sense of security.

I didn't tell you exactly what was going on when we took that trip to the Georgia mountains. You and your friend played outside the restaurant while his mom and I visited the ladies room. Later, the two of you told us that a white man and his wife—he with a minister's collar—stared at you "with mean looks" and made monkey sounds and gestures. You asked why they did that, and I told you that some people were just not very nice. I made you promise to come to me immediately for help whenever an adult was giving you any trouble.

You don't know yet why I am so reluctant to let you go out of town with your white friends. Do you remember when you went with Knox and his mom to Chattanooga? When the car had a flat tire, the reason no one would help his mom is because you, my brown angel, were with them. She told me some of the comments made on those Georgia highways, and I cannot bring myself to let you know what hostility is out there in the world waiting to attack that lovely sense of confidence you carry in your every step.

I did not have to be told much when I was your age. When I was growing up in Louisiana in the 1950s and '60s, the color lines were very clearly drawn. With few explanations beyond the age of three or four, I understood that television characters like Buckskin Bill and Miss Pat of Romper Room didn't mean me when they told children to ask their parents to bring them down to the studio to be a part of the television audience. I followed my mother to the back entrance of the doctor's office, marked "colored." I knew which water fountain I was supposed to drink from. On the bus ride to my all-black school, I watched white children walk to schools just two or three blocks from my house, and I never learned to swim because rather than integrate the all-white swimming pools, the city chose to close all its pools for years at a time.

In large part, my childhood years were wrapped in the warm cocoon of family and community who all knew each other and looked out for one another. However, whenever people of different colors came together outside of the "normal" realm of black/white interactions, there was likely to be trouble. I remember clearly my racing heart, my sweaty-palmed fear of the white policemen who entered my father's small restaurant one night and hit him with nightsticks, the helpless terror when there were rumors in our school yard that the Ku Klux Klan would be riding, the worried anxiety of knowing my college-aged foster sister had joined the civil rights marchers in a face-off against the white policemen and their dogs. And I remember, my Maya, the death of your grandfather when I was seven. Although I didn't know the details until much, much later, he died of kidney failure because the "colored" ward wasn't yet allowed the use of the brand new dialysis machine.

Your world is very different, at least on its surface. In many ways now is a more confusing time to live. In *Seeing a Colorblind Future*, Patricia Williams says we are saturated with insistent emblems of brotherhood—multicolored children singing "We are the World"; television shows with the obligatory child of color (although seldom in the lead role); teachers' adamant statements to their classes that "we are all the same" and "color doesn't matter." Yet, attacks on rectifying past discrimination are made unabashedly under the flag of "color-blindness," white hate crimes are on the upswing, many communities and schools are more segregated than they were twenty years ago. I receive at least a call a week from frantic African American parents living all over the country who are terrified at the only slightly hostilily shown regularly by the schools to their brown children. And my nine-year-old child is stopped by the police every time she walks her dog.

As any mother would, I have a great need to protect you, but it is hard to know how. My childhood experience was different from yours in other ways, too. As was the case in many African American Louisiana families, our family was a rainbow of colors, from chocolate-brown brunettes to peach-colored blondes. (The history of that reality is a story we'll need to talk about later.) I was the light-skinned, freckled, red-headed child, who always got the sunburn whenever we went to the beach. Because of my coloring, I had another role, too. When traveling by car, African Americans were not allowed to use the restrooms or other facilities white travellers took for granted. Black families had to develop all sorts of strategies to make a road trip workable. When it was time for a rest stop, one of our ruses was to pull around to the side of the service station and send in the one who looked most like white to get the key. Then, outside of the attendant's view, everyone would use the facility.

So, you see, although I was enmeshed within an African American family, in some ways I also lived on the "border"—not easily identifiable to hostile outsiders, able to sometimes slip between the jagged, dangerous bars of the segregated prisons we were all, black and white, forced to inhabit. Decades later, when you were an infant, your aunt and I drove to Mississippi. I had not made that trip for many years, and although segregation was officially over, I still felt uneasy at the rest stops. Any African American would. There were Confederate flags printed on every possible souvenir in the gift shops, and the restaurants and gas stations were filled with burly, white, cigarette-smoking men with gun racks mounted in their rear windows. More Confederate flags decorated the doors of their pick-ups, their license plates, and their upper arms. Heart racing, cradling my beautiful brown baby, I suddenly realized for the first time that the borders in which I could previously find anonymous refuge were gone; the bars I could slip through were welded into an impenetrable wall. We were revealed, and I did not know how to protect you from the vicious hatred in some of the eyes that stared at us. Or, for that matter, from a society whose very structure privileges some and marginalizes you.

Although I still cannot protect you from the outside forces, I have tried to protect you from the disease of internalized racism—of seeing yourself through the eyes of those who disdain you—that infects the souls of so many of our young people. When I was in my segregated, all-black elementary school, we were told by teachers and parents that we had to excel, that we had to "do better than" any white kids because the world was already on their side. Just six short years later, your cousin Joey completed all his schooling in predominantly white settings. By the time he was in high school, I remember berating him for getting a "D" in chemistry. His response was, "What do you expect of me, the white kids get 'C's.'" Recently a colleague tried to help an African American middle-schooler to learn multiplication. The student looked up at the teacher and said, "Why are you trying to teach me this? Black people don't multiply. Black people just add and subtract. Multiplication is for white people." You know, Maya, I think that may be the biggest challenge you and other brown children will face—not believing the limits that others place upon you.

It is not easy to know how to keep you believing in yourself, even believing in your abundant radiance and beauty. When you were very little, you, like all small children, wanted to own the children's videos popular at the time. I resisted, fearing a steady diet of *Cinderella, Sleeping Beauty, The Little Mermaid*, and *Snow White* would only reinforce our society's limited notion of beauty as white skin, blue eyes, and long silky hair. I searched all over for children's films reflecting your physical attributes, but to no avail. Now, Disney has created videos with a Roma "Gypsy" heroine (*Esmeralda*), an East Indian heroine (*Jasmine*), a Native American heroine (*Pocahontas*), and a

Chinese heroine (*Mulan*). But I suspect we will have to wait until you are a mother before we have hopes of getting from them an animated African or African American heroine.

Every year at Christmas time I took you to the one mall with the African American Santa. I told you that he was the "real" Santa and the white ones all around were his assistants. I also searched for beautiful brown dolls, and sometimes found them, but noticed that somehow white manufacturers had a way of merely creating brown-tinted dolls with the same white-doll features. Even then, they would sometimes still find a way to devalue the supposed black doll: The white-skinned Barbie was billed as "Glamour Queen Barbie," while her identical-in-every-way-other-than-skin-tone counterpart was merely listed as "Black Barbie."

When you wanted to look just like me, and then just like Snow White, I told you how much I envied your beautiful brown skin, and how Snow White really wished she could have skin like yours so she could also look so beautiful in the sun. When you wanted to have hair like your white classmates, I pointed out to you how many more styles your hair could accommodate and how soft it felt, just like cotton candy. I know there was a time when you couldn't understand why I wouldn't allow you to wear a white character mask at Halloween, or why I told your grandmother to stop sending you white dolls.

It's hard for a mother to know just how far to go with principles, though. And I think you helped me develop a somewhat less strident attitude in your own brilliant, unpredictable way. I remember refusing to buy a white Barbie—even though the store didn't have the black one with equivalent turn-colors-in-the-sun hair. You were not happy with me, even though I explained at length the reasons I had regarding not bringing dolls into our family who looked like they could not possibly *be* a part of our family. "You don't see any of your white friends begging for black Barbie dolls, do you?" I asked, adding what I thought would be the final word. You said nothing more at the time, but several days later in another conversation, asked, "Mom, do you have any white friends?" "Of course, I do, Maya, you know that," I answered quickly. "Do you like your white friends, Mom?" "What a question, Maya, if they're my friends, then I like them." "Well, Mom," you delivered your knock-out punch, "my black Barbies want some white friends, too." Well, my dear, from that moment on your doll collection became interracial, but to your (and my, I hope) credit, you will usually still choose a brown doll unless there is some particular reason not to.

It is so hard to know how both to engender the possibility of color not mattering—where people will truly be judged not by the color of their skin, but the content of their character—and to give you understandings that will create a protective armor for the real world of racial bias that exists around you. I don't want to limit you, to make you wonder if there are places and spaces that are not as much for you as for others, to have you always on edge (as I sometimes feel) questioning the intentions of white playmates or teachers. Decisions based on color are so pervasive, and people of color so demonized in this country—though racist comments are often thinly camouflaged by such terms as "teen-aged mother," "the criminal element", "welfare cheaters," "drug dealers," "school drop-outs," "at-risk students" — that understanding societal realities does not come as easily as it did in my childhood. In conversations about racial bias with white colleagues, they are as likely as not to suggest that African Americans are being "too emotional," or even "picky."

Like it or not, you will not have the same experience in this country as your white classmates or our white neighbors. In this country we are marked as part of a stigmatized group, and many are ready to attribute any characteristic they ascribe to our group to either of us. Our middle-class standing will help some, but neither the police nor violent racists will stop to find out who your mother is or where you live or what your achievement test scores were.

Recently, there was a movie on television that purported to be a comedy. The central gag was that a black Nobel Laureate moves into a formerly all-white neighborhood. When the neighbors see him carrying his stereo equipment, they call the police, who assume he has taken the "real" home owner hostage and begin firing at him and later accuse him of murder. There's a tasteless, but nonetheless apparently timeless old joke that goes, "What do you call a black man with a Ph.D. in America?" And the answer is—"Nigger."

Yes, Maya, I really do want to believe that a color-blind future is possible. So I don't tell you that the police weren't just being friendly, and I haven't told you why it took so long to get that flat tire fixed, and I haven't let you know how truly cruel that "minister" was being to two small brown children. I also never express my doubts when one of the parents at your school calls me at the last minute to invite you to a birthday party, adding that "Suzie [whom you hardly know and seldom play with, but who is the only other black girl in your class] is coming."

The afternoon following last Halloween, you and your two buddies bolted into the house with sheepish looks and a bag of candy telling me you had decided to try for a second round of trick-or-treating. As I understood the tale, one woman smiled and gave the three of you her leftover candy. A second woman saw three black nine-year-old faces, screamed at you and immediately called the police. You three were quite a muddle of emotions— delight with the additional candy and real fear at the thought of the "mean lady" and the police. I was furious, but after telling you all that post-Halloween trick-or-treating was *not a good idea*, I only added that some people just don't have a sense of humor and that the woman probably didn't have any more candy left anyway.

I am proud yet torn when I hear you come to some understandings on your own. Like when you were two and you stroked the arm of one of our white friends gently and said in a sympathetic voice, "Oh, poor Barbara, you don't have brown skin." Or when you were seven and playing in the back seat of the car with a little friend who had brought his cowboy and Indian figures, and you said, "Ok, I'll be the Indians and you be the bad guys." Or when you went bike-riding with a friend and came back upset that "a white boy"—as opposed to just "a boy"— said he was going to hurt you. Or when you asked me why there weren't any black teachers in your school and added that you hoped that the school "didn't think black people weren't as smart as white people." When I told you that you needed to talk to the principal about that, you went right up to her the next day and asked your question. She, to her credit, took your question seriously and explained that they would like to find more black teachers, but that the salaries the school paid made it hard to attract them. Not one to let anyone off easy, you immediately came back with, "Well, have you tried Morehouse?"[16]

I am pleased that you have realized that brown skin is good, that cowboys weren't always good, that the boy who threatened you may have done so, not because of anything *you* did, but because *he* had a problem with color that had nothing to do with your worth, and that it is good to question authorities about issues of equity. Yet, I am saddened that you cannot be innocent to the unfortunate realities surrounding you. You have understood that the color line lives.

I know what can happen when African American or other children of color grow up without these understandings. Those children, raised in white neighborhoods, attending predominantly white schools, learn to believe the story that color doesn't matter. Eventually, they are *always* faced with situations where it does. Sometimes it comes in high school when dates are hard to come by, or when assumptions are made about who stole the missing money or who knocked over the neighbor's mailboxes. Sometimes it doesn't come until college when some sorority or fraternity won't grant them admission, or someone mistakes them for the maid, or a professor assumes that all black students need tutoring help. I have seen what happens when this understanding comes late, and it is ugly. These young people are devastated. Frequently they internalize the rejection and feel that it is their problem, something *they* have done to cause the response they get from others. I have seen many so disillusioned when they finally understand that we do not, indeed, function in a meritocracy, that they drop out of school altogether, coming to believe that the struggle just isn't worth it.

I don't want that for you, Maya. Yet, neither do I want you always looking over your shoulder wondering whether every hardship or slight has racial overtones. I want desperately to let you believe in the possibility of a future in which color doesn't matter, although I cannot help but wonder if that reality will ever come to pass. I wouldn't be able to stand it if one day you looked me in the eye with a pained accusatory look and said—as you did when I finally debunked another myth and admitted that Santa Claus doesn't really leave the Christmas presents—"But, Mom, why didn't you *tell* me?"

Love you always,

Mom

Afterword

TAHAR BEN JELLOUN

EVERYTHING I KNOW about the United States comes from film, jazz, and fiction. As a teenager in Tangiers, I managed to convince my parents that a movie was as educational as a history or geography class. We were lucky enough to have two movie theaters right next to our school; each showed a different film daily. I learned about American film in those theaters with their wooden seats, dirty screens, and sporadic darkness. A blackboard served as the marquee, touting the virtues of that day's film: "Action!" "Emotion!" "Ten fights!" "Five kissing scenes!"

I loved westerns, especially when the hero chased the bad guys out of town. The "bad guys" were mostly Indians. I remember movies in which the Indians would attack white settlements. They would steal up in the night, massacre everyone, and escape back to their mountain camps after having scalped several of their enemies. I found this terrifying, because I identified with the children of the white frontiersmen. To me, the Indians were lawless pagans. That is how the facts were presented, and I accepted them. No one had taught me the history of Native Americans. I was ignorant. And by virtue of this ignorance, I was racist.

In those days, the American movie industry saw itself as the defender of Good in the struggle against Evil. Evil nearly always lay on the same side, namely that of the Indians, blacks, or cantankerous indigents motivated by hunger or alcoholism. Later I would discover another American cinema, one that was humanistic, subtle, and antiracist.

I was bowled over by Delmer Daves's 1950 film, *Broken Arrow*. It was the first time an American had tried to help the Indians. They were no longer savage scalpers or aggressive warriors, but oppressed human beings who had been denied the right to live on their land according to their customs. In my mind, nothing would ever be the same. The cinema had an obligation to take the victim's side and to defend the weak and dispossessed. I became a pro-Indian militant and began to seek out information on their history.

Some time later I saw Samuel Fuller's *Run of the Arrow* (1956), which also portrayed Indians positively. The film was set during the War between the States. To escape the savage violence of the northern troops, a Confederate soldier joined the Sioux, whom he found to be very human. As in Delmer Daves's film, the Indians were presented as human beings fighting for the survival of their community, and for the recovery of lands taken from them by whites.

Films by John Ford, Antony Mann, Raoul Walsh, and others followed. I came to understand that the Indians were victims of putative white supremacy and had been deprived of their property for racist reasons. The Spaniards had already distinguished themselves with the same form of genocide.

With regard to blacks, the American cinema took its time before beginning to make movies denouncing discrimination and racist laws, paralleling the slow development of social attitudes. I remember a black-and-white film in which Rock Hudson escapes from prison with a fellow prisoner played by Sidney Poitier. The two are chained together. The film forces the viewer to think about the prospects for coexistence between the two groups, blacks and whites. The violent demonstrations against racial segregation in Alabama in 1968 had a powerful effect on me. I discovered that the great notion of American democracy had major problems. Children with black skin did not have the right to swim in the same pools as children with white skin. I learned that people of different colors could not marry. In 1966, at least nineteen states still had legislation forbidding mixed marriages (including Alabama, Arkansas, Florida, Idaho, and Louisiana). I remember Stanley Kramer's film, *Guess Who's Coming to Dinner?* with Spencer Tracy and Sidney Poitier, and *The Heat of the Night*, by Norman Jewisson (1967), in which the investigator was a black officer.

I never understood how such a great nation could have grown in power while committing horrible injustices such as the massacre of the Indians and the enslavement of the blacks. The story of the great blues singer Bessie Smith comes to mind. She was denied medical care when she tried to enter a hospital for whites. I later heard the unbelievable story of black Americans with syphilis who were denied the right to penicillin treatment. This happened at the end of the 1930s, when doctors in Washington, D.C., decided to use black patients as guinea pigs to see if blacks had better immune systems than whites.

William Faulkner's *Intruder in the Dust* also comes to mind. That novel examines racism in the context of a crime in which prejudice overcomes truth and reason.

American society does not seem to have waited for criticism before beginning to deal frankly with its own problems. Racism and violence against Native Americans, blacks, and hispanics is now condemned in movies, literature, and other media.

The very fact that a society composed of several waves of immigration today acknowledges the importance of its minorities, that there is not one American culture but several, and that the civil rights of nonwhites are recognized, helps America fight the growth of racism. As in any society rich in diversity and complexity, it has its fanatics, such as the Ku Klux Klan, infamous for their hate for "impure races."

Racism is everywhere, and there is no reason why the United States should be the only society in the world to be free of it. Not only is racism present, but it constantly crops up anew, abetted by new communications technologies and democratic freedoms. Thanks to movies, music, and culture, however, the stupidity of racism is just as constantly denounced. Today, the American imagination embraces multiple representations of the various segments of society. On television and in advertising, especially, one finds the full diversity of the human landscape of this immense country. People can learn to live together. The images we take in every day no longer depict the supposed purity of the white male, domineering and self-assured.

OCTOBER 1998

ABOUT THE CONTRIBUTORS

WILLIAM AYERS is Professor of Education and Senior University Scholar at the University of Illinois at Chicago where he teaches courses in interpretive research, urban crisis, teaching for justice and democracy, youth and the modern predicament, and the cultural contexts of young people's lives. A graduate of Bank Street College of Education and Teachers College, Columbia University, he has written extensively about urban education and policy. His articles have appeared in many journals including the *Harvard Educational Review*, *The Nation*, and *The Cambridge Journal of Education.* His books include *The Good Preschool Teacher* (Teachers College Press, 1989) *To Teach: The Journey of a Teacher* (Teachers College Press, 1993), which was named Book of the Year in 1993 by Kappa Delta Pi and won the Witten Award for Distinguished Work in Biography and Autobiography in 1995; *City Kids, City Teachers: Reports from the Front Row* (edited with Patricia Ford, The New Press, 1996); and *A Kind and Just Parent: The Children of Juvenile Court* (Beacon Press, 1997). His latest book is *Teaching for Social Justice: A Democracy and Education Reader* (1998) edited with Therese Quinn and Jean Ann Hunt, published jointly by Teachers College Press and The New Press. He is the father of three—Zayd, 21, Malik, 18, and Chesa, 18—and lives with Bernadine Dohrn in Hyde Park, Chicago.

LISA D. DELPIT is the holder of the Benjamin E. Mays Chair of Urban Educational Excellence at Georgia State University, Atlanta, Georgia. Originally from Baton Rouge,

Louisiana, she is a nationally and internationally-known speaker and writer whose work has focused on the education of children of color and the perspectives, aspirations, and pedagogical knowledge of teachers of color. She has used her training in ethnographic research to spark dialogues between educators on issues which impact students typically least well-served by our educational system. Dr. Delpit is particularly interested in teaching and learning in multicultural societies, having spent time studying these issues in Alaska, Papua New Guinea, Fiji, and in various urban and rural sites in the United States. Her background is in elementary education with an emphasis on language and literacy development. Her recent work has spanned a range of projects and issues, including creating high-standards, innovative schools for poor, urban children, and developing urban leadership programs for teachers. She has also taught preservice and inservice teachers in many communities across the United States. Her primary effort at this time is establishing the Center for Urban Educational Excellence at Georgia State. Delpit's work on school-community relations and cross-cultural communication were cited as contributions to her receiving a MacArthur "Genius" Award in 1990. Dr. Delpit describes her strongest focus as "finding ways and means to best educate urban students, particularly African American, and other students of color."

BILL COSBY, one of America's most beloved stars, is executive producer of "Cosby" and stars in the series. He also hosts "Kids Say The Darndest Things" on CBS. Through concert appearances, records, television, feature films, books, and commercials, Cosby has touched people's lives.

He is now entering his third year as the star of "Cosby," which received the 1996 People's Choice Award as America's Favorite New Television Comedy Series.

Cosby was on the nightclub circuit when he made the transition from standup comic to actor as co-star of the series "I Spy," with Robert Culp. Cosby won three Emmy Awards as Best Actor for the role, which was instrumental in breaking racial barriers in American television. His additional television credits include "The Bill Cosby Show," the variety show "Cos," and the hit comedy series "The Cosby Show," which also starred his current television wife, Phylicia Rashad.

Cosby produced the series "A Different World" with the team of Marcy Carsey and Tom Werner.

Cosby's successful recording career began with *Bill Cosby Is a Very Funny Fellow, Right?* His many subsequent comedy albums earned him a total of five Grammy Awards in the category of Best Comedy Album. He has also released a number of jazz recordings, including *hello, friend: to ennis with love*, in 1997.

Cosby is the author of *little bill*, a book series designed to encourage reading among children ages six through ten. The bestselling books are being developed into a television series.

He is the author of the books *Fatherhood* and *Time Flies*, both record-breaking bestsellers, and the bestseller *Childhood*.

Cosby received his bachelor's degree from Temple University in Philadelphia. He earned a master's degree from the University of Massachusetts in 1972, and earned a doctorate in education there in 1977. In addition to his involvement with a host of charitable organizations, Cosby remains an active trustee of Temple University.

He was born in Philadelphia. He and his wife, Camille (née Hanks), are the parents of four daughters, Erika, Erinn, Ensa, and Evin, and one son, the late Ennis.

TAHAR BEN JELLOUN

Born in 1944, the son of a Fez shopkeeper, author Tahar Ben Jelloun grew up in a traditional Muslim household and was educated in bilingual French/Arabic schools. He studied philosophy at the University of Rabat, and taught in Morocco for three years following his military service. In 1971, Ben Jelloun moved to Paris, where he received a doctorate in psychiatry. A regular contributor to periodicals including *Le Monde*, *La Répubblica*, *El Pais* and *Panorama*, he lives in Paris with his wife and four children. Tahar Ben Jelloun is the first North African to win the Prix Goncourt, France's equivalent of the National Book Award, for his novel *The Sacred Night* in 1987. Winner of the 1994 Prix Maghreb, Ben Jelloun is described as one of the most acclaimed novelists writing in French today. His novel, *Corruption*, was published by The New Press in 1996. Novels published in English include *The Sand Child* (Harcourt Brace Jovanovich), *Silent Day in Tangier* (Harcourt Brace Jovanovich), *With Downcast Eyes* (Time Warner), and *State of Absence*. Ben Jelloun's other works include novels (*Harrouda*, 1973; *Moha le fou, Moha le sage*, 1978; *La Prière de l'absent*, 1981; *La Réclusion solitaire*, 1981; *L'Ecrivain public*, 1983; *Le Premier amour est toujours le dernier*, 1995; *Les Raisins de la galère*, 1996; *La*

Nuit de l'erreur, 1997; *L'Auberge des pauvres*, 1999), essays ("La Plus haute des solitudes. Misères affective et sexuelle d'émigrés nord-africains," 1977; "Hospitalité française. Racisme et immigration maghrébine," 1984; "Giacometti," 1991; "La Soudure frater-nelle,"1994; poetry ("Les Amandiers sont morts de leurs blessures," 1976; "La Remontée des cendres," 1991; "Poésie com-plète," 1995), *L'Ange aveugle* (1992), a novella, and plays ("Entre-tien avec Saïd Hamadi," "La Fiancée de l'eau").

DAVID MURA is a poet, creative nonfiction writer, critic, play-wright, and performance artist. A Sansei, or third-generation Japanese-American, Mura has written two memoirs: *Turning Japanese: Memoirs of a Sansei* (Anchor Doubleday), which won a Josephine Miles Book Award from the Oakland PEN and was listed in the *New York Times* Notable Books of the Year, and *Where the Body Meets Memory: An Odyssey of Race, Sexuality, and Identity* (1996, Anchor Doubleday).

Mura's most recent book of poetry, *The Colors of Desire* (1995, Anchor), won the Carl Sandburg Literary Award from the friends of the Chicago Public Library. His first, *After We Lost Our Way* (Carnegie Mellon University Press), won the 1989 National Poetry Series Contest. He has also written *A Male Grief: Notes on Pornography and Addiction* (Milkweed Editions). He is currently working on a novel loosely based on the life of Isamu Noguchi.

Along with African American writer Alexs Pate, Mura has created and performs a multi-media performance piece, *Secret Colors*, about their lives as men of color and Asian American-African American relations. This piece premiered for the Walker

Art Center, Minneapolis (1994) and has been presented at various venues throughout the country. A film adaptation of this piece, *Slowly, This,* was broadcast in the PBS series "Alive TV" in July/August 1995. Mura has also been featured on the Bill Moyers PBS series, "The Language of Life."

He gives readings and speaks on the issues of race and multiculturism throughout the country. He lives in Minneapolis with his wife and three children, Samantha, Nikko, and Tomo.

PATRICIA J. WILLIAMS is a Professor of Law at Columbia University School of Law. A graduate of Wellesley College and Harvard Law School, she has served on faculties of the University of Wisconsin School of Law, Harvard University Women's Studies Program, and the City University of New York Law School at Queen's College. She is the recipient of an Honorary Doctorate of Law from Northeastern University.

Before entering academia, she practiced law, as a consumer advocate and deputy city attorney for the City of Los Angeles, and as a staff attorney for the Western Center on Law and Poverty.

She serves on the board of the National Organization for Women Legal Defense and Education Fund and authors the column "Diary of a Mad Law Professor" for *The Nation*. She has authored numerous articles for scholarly journals and popular magazines and newspapers including the *New York Times, USA Today, Harvard Law Review, Tikkun,* the *New York Times Book Review, The Nation, Ms. Magazine, The New Yorker,* and the *Village Voice*. Her book *The Alchemy of Race and Rights* (Harvard University Press, 1995) was named one of the twenty-two best books of 1991 by the *Voice Literary Supplement* (Dec. 10, 1991, p. 16-17), and one of the "feminist classics of the last twenty years" that "literally changed women's lives," by *Ms. Magazine*'s Twentieth Anniversary Edition (July/August 1992, p. 64). Her other books include *The Rooster's Egg* (Harvard University Press, 1995) and *Seeing a Color-blind Future: The Paradox of Race* (Farrar, Straus & Giroux, 1998).

She has appeared on a variety of radio and television shows, including "Charlie Rose" (PBS), "The MacNeil-Lehrer News Hour" (PBS), "All Things Considered" (NPR), "Fresh Air with Terri Gross" (NPR), "Talk of the Nation" (NPR), "Crier and Company" (CNN), "The Today Show" (NBC), and the "Pozner-Donahue Show" (NBC).